MORE PRAISE FOR *WISCONSIN IDOLS*

"Dean Robbins's collection of brief essays is a passionate and poetic homage to one hundred musicians, artists, thinkers, entertainers, and athletes (including me) whose presence, however brief or long, in his beloved Wisconsin impacted the state and him. It's both insightful and entertaining."

—Kareem Abdul-Jabbar, *National Basketball Association hall-of-famer*

◊˘◊˘◊

"Lucky me, I'm included in Dean Robbins's wonderful, skillfully written book. I had no idea that many of these extraordinary people had Wisconsin connections. *Wisconsin Idols* is artful, thoughtful, and sharp-sighted—and it's bursting with interesting facts and one fascinating anecdote after another."

—Kevin Henkes, *Caldecott Medal–winning children's author*

◊˘◊˘◊

"Not only are the stories in *Wisconsin Idols* inspiring, exhilarating and moving—they gave me a whole new way of seeing this state. Not just as a collection of towns and streets and gentle hills, but as a landscape of stories, inhabited by the traces of legendary makers, creators, doers, and thinkers. I'll never travel Wisconsin again without wondering "what happened here?" and "who lived there?" This is place-making at its finest. What an absolute gift."

—Anne Strainchamps, *Peabody Award–winning host and cocreator of the National Public Radio program* To the Best of Our Knowledge

◊˘◊˘◊

"I loved being a 1950s student at the University of Wisconsin–Madison, where my professional writing career began. Now, thanks to Dean Robbins's *Wisconsin Idols*, I've belatedly discovered Wisconsin's cultural richness. It's a fascinating, sharply written index to his mind, and just as important, a reminder that the USA is not just a union of states, but a union of cultural streams, fascinating people, and high achievers. These are people you need to know, from cultural icons to unknowns who should be known. On Wisconsin!"

—Avi, *Newbery Medal–winning children's author*

◊⁻◊⁻◊

"Dean Robbins's *Wisconsin Idols* combines a youthfully innocent wonder at the magic of stardom with a seasoned journalist's incisive analysis of what makes these stars so remarkable—and how they are linked in some way to Wisconsin. The result is one hundred snapshots that range widely, including some greats you've probably never heard of, all told with a born storyteller's vision and verve. It's a great read."

—Bruce Murphy, *editor and award-winning columnist,* Urban Milwaukee

Wisconsin Idols

100 Heroes Who Changed the State, the World, and Me

Dean Robbins

WISCONSIN HISTORICAL SOCIETY PRESS

Published by the Wisconsin Historical Society Press
Publishers since 1855

The Wisconsin Historical Society helps people connect to the past by collecting, preserving, and sharing stories. Founded in 1846, the Society is one of the nation's finest historical institutions.
Join the Wisconsin Historical Society: wisconsinhistory.org/membership

Photographs identified with WHI or WHS are from the Society's collections; address requests to reproduce these photos to the Visual Materials Archivist at the Wisconsin Historical Society, 816 State Street, Madison, WI 53706.

Front cover images: Top row, left to right: Justin Vernon (Wikimedia Commons), Richard Davis (University of Wisconsin–Madison Archives, photo by Brent Nicastro), Oprah Winfrey (Wikimedia Commons), Kareem Abdul-Jabbar (Wikimedia Commons). Bottom row, left to right: Chris Farley (Wisconsin Center for Film and Theater Research), Laurel Clark (NASA), Mountain Wolf Woman (WHI IMAGE ID 60939).

Printed in the United States of America
Cover design by Tom Heffron
Typesetting by Integrated Composition Systems
29 28 27 26 25   1 2 3 4 5

Library of Congress Cataloging-in-Publication Data
Names: Robbins, Dean, 1957– author.
Title: Wisconsin idols : 100 heroes who changed the state, the world, and me / Dean Robbins.
Other titles: 100 heroes who changed the state, the world, and me
Description: [Madison, WI] : Wisconsin Historical Society Press, [2025] |
  Includes bibliographical references and index.
Identifiers: LCCN 2024034760 (print) | LCCN 2024034761 (ebook) |
  ISBN 9781976600470 (paperback) | ISBN 9781976600487 (ebook)
Subjects: LCSH: Wisconsin—Biography. | Wisconsin—Miscellanea.
Classification: LCC F580 .R63 2025 (print) | LCC F580 (ebook) |
  DDC 977.50099—dc23/eng/20241203
LC record available at https://lccn.loc.gov/2024034760
LC ebook record available at https://lccn.loc.gov/2024034761

For Ann and Jo

Contents

THINKERS

Preface

Cheating Death in Appleton

I had a single thought when I moved to Wisconsin at age twenty-three: *Harry Houdini.*

As a boy in St. Louis, I'd obsessed over the world's greatest escape artist, and I knew he'd spent part of his nineteenth-century childhood in Appleton. The city was just two hours from my new home in Madison, close enough for a Houdini daytrip. Nothing—not handcuffs, chains, or straitjackets—could keep me from walking in his footsteps along the Fox River, where a near-drowning incident had sparked his lifelong interest in cheating death. And what a thrill to stroll near his onetime home off College Avenue, where he'd begun devising the tricks that would transform him from a small-timer to a superstar.

Little did I know that I would soon make many similar pilgrimages. As a Madison-based journalist, I discovered figures who performed extraordinary feats throughout Wisconsin, from Oshkosh to Eau Claire, Racine to Richland Center. They were writers and musicians, politicians and painters, athletes and astronauts, soldiers and scientists, and even a movie star renowned for thirteen seconds on screen. Some you might recognize as legendary residents: Bart Starr, Hank Aaron, Spencer Tracy, Chris Farley, Justin Vernon, Kareem Abdul-Jabbar. And some you might not: Oprah Winfrey, Georgia O'Keeffe, Harrison Ford, Jim Lovell, Liberace, Lorraine Hansberry, Ann Landers, Abigail Van Buren. Others had a significant experience while passing through, including the Beatles, Elvis Presley, Bob Dylan, Kurt Cobain, Duke Ellington, and Little Richard. This book establishes Wisconsin as a notably influential state: a crossroads for people who changed the world.

Together at last: the author communes with his idol Harry Houdini in
Appleton in 2022. PHOTO BY ANN SHAFFER

    I've been collecting personal heroes since second grade, when I
saw a TV broadcast of the 1953 biopic *Houdini*. I marveled over the
magician's penchant for busting out of sealed crates and coffins and,
in homage, I spent hours wriggling out of towels I'd directed my
sister to tie tightly around my wrists and ankles. With Houdini, I

established a process I would follow with countless other idols: reading their biographies, hanging their posters on my bedroom wall, and trying to figure out what made them tick.

After I settled in Wisconsin and took that first trip to Appleton, I sought out other locations in the state associated with my heroes. Visiting such places proved, to my satisfaction, that these awe-inspiring individuals truly had lived among us. When I read about Houdini, or watched Tony Curtis play him in that 1953 movie, he seemed mythic. But when I saw the actual building where his dad had worked—and where, he once said, "I used to get my spankings"—the myth seemed human.[1] Maybe even someone I could emulate.

I'm not saying I aspire to be *exactly* like Houdini. He had his good and not-so-good qualities, like everyone in this book—and everyone who's ever lived. But even with their flaws, I regard all the subjects in *Wisconsin Idols* as inspirational in some way. Each of them has a tale I love to tell.

I've divided the book's subjects into the categories of Melody Makers, Creators, Scene Stealers, Champs, Boundary Breakers, and Thinkers. You might wonder why an idea man like architect Frank Lloyd Wright is a Creator rather than a Thinker or why a showboat like Orson Welles is a Creator rather than a Scene Stealer. You might also wonder what the likes of Joni Mitchell, Abraham Lincoln, and Jackie Robinson are even doing here, given that they spent mere hours in the state. I say, read on—and if you disagree with any of my choices, I'm happy to defend them over fried cheese curds at the Up-North supper club of your choice.

Obviously, Wisconsin history has more than a few dozen heroic figures. I've chosen the ones whose narratives most move me and whose posters I'd place on my wall next to Houdini's. I've been lucky enough to interview some for newspaper or magazine articles—and I truly wish I could have spoken to everyone in this book, from beyond the grave if necessary.

As an essayist and critic, I can't help but present an entirely subjective view of these icons. I also couldn't resist inserting myself into some of their stories. Having dreamed of and doted on them for so many years, I tend to think of their lives as inseparable from my own.

   If *Wisconsin Idols* makes you yearn to visit Appleton in search of Houdini—or to visit Kenosha, Ashland, Green Bay, Janesville, and La Crosse in search of other heroes you find here—I'll feel I've done my job. And if it makes you yearn to wriggle out of towels tied tightly around your wrists and ankles, all I can say is: welcome to the club.

Melody Makers

1

Joni Mitchell

A Mystical Moment

The 1970s were an age of journeys. Kids like me hitchhiked, hopped trains, and headed back to nature. Joni Mitchell lit the way.

Like us, Mitchell was—to quote fellow '70s singer-songwriter Cat Stevens—on the road to find out. Right before our eyes, she transformed from the open-hearted folkie of "Chelsea Morning" to the jaded romantic of "River" to the brash pop star of "Help Me." In 1976, her wanderlust brought her to Madison and a spontaneous photo shoot on frozen Lake Mendota. The photographs later appeared on an album, encapsulating Joni's personal odyssey as well as a whole generation's.

Mitchell arrived in Madison during an ice storm and played a February 29 concert at the Dane County Coliseum. She'd just broken up with her longtime boyfriend and called off the rest of her troubled tour, so she felt even bluer than "Blue." Gazing at Lake Mendota from the Edgewater Hotel, she heard the call of the glassy white void. Tree branches cracked under the weight of the ice, a sound reminiscent of tinkling glass.

Mitchell bought a pair of men's black skates on State Street, donned a long black skirt and a black ermine cape, and leaped onto the ice. The surface proved dangerously spongy, and freezing water splashed onto her face. But she went through with the impulsive plan. Her photographer followed along to record the scene.

Mitchell found that her cape acted as a sort of sail. She spread her arms and let the wind carry her, looking like a crow in flight. The photographs captured a mystical moment: an artist on an unearthly journey, destination unknown and arrival uncertain.

Joni liked the photos so much that she incorporated them into a black-and-white montage on her 1976 album *Hejira*. The title is an Arabic word meaning "journey," and the wintry images perfectly fit the musical message. Chilled by jazz-rock guitar, the songs are less melodies than moods. They're less pop than poetry. In "Coyote," "Amelia," and other meandering masterworks, Mitchell evokes the restlessness of the road, mirroring that of her soul. Jaco Pastorius's prodding bass seems like a stand-in for her nagging psychic obsessions.

On *Rolling Stone*'s 1991 list of the one hundred greatest album covers, *Hejira* came in eleventh. For Madison residents, however, the imagery carries special meaning. It shows that Lake Mendota is not only a body of water but also something far more mysterious: an expanse of endless possibility.

2

The Beatles

All Their Loving

The Beatles made their sole Wisconsin appearance on September 4, 1964, amid pure chaos. The madness started the minute their plane touched down in Milwaukee's Mitchell Field, with eighty stern police officers keeping watch.

This was the Liverpool lads' first US tour, and hundreds of young fans showed up to swoon and sigh in their presence. But the police wanted nothing of the sort, so they directed the plane to land far away from the crowd. Then they hustled the musicians through a back exit, preventing the fans from even glimpsing a mop top or a Beatle boot.

The band protested to no avail. Later, at a press conference, bassist Paul McCartney accused the police of pulling "a dirty trick" to keep them from greeting their fans. And that was just the start of the Beatles' pushback against these disapproving members of the older generation. When a reporter posed the same insulting question everyone was asking during their *Hard Day's Night* period—"What will you do when the bubble bursts?"—guitarist George Harrison deadpanned, "Ice hockey."[1]

Tickets for the concert at Milwaukee Arena topped out at the going rate of $5.50. At showtime, Red Cross workers positioned themselves around the venue to treat fainting teens. As for the performance, twelve thousand euphoric Beatlemaniacs mostly drowned it out. What with all the screaming, few could tell "All My Loving" from "I Want to Hold Your Hand." Nevertheless, the Beatles sang with abandon and playfully engaged the crowd between numbers. In news accounts, attendees spoke of the

At their Milwaukee press conference in 1964, the Beatles blamed police
for pulling "a dirty trick." Left to right: John Lennon, Paul McCartney,
and George Harrison. WHI IMAGE ID 102185

experience with awe, and the conversation continues to this day on
Beatles blogs.

Before the Fab Four left town on September 5, McCartney took
time to call a fan in the hospital, having heard she'd missed the show.
The band may have scorned Wisconsin's clueless elders, but they
cared deeply about the kids who cared about them.

A half-century later, I saw a Beatle myself in Milwaukee.
McCartney played a sold-out solo show at Miller Park, with ticket
prices well over $5.50.

In many ways, the performance recalled the Beatles' Milwaukee
Arena concert of 1964. Once again, Paul playfully engaged the
crowd. And, even at age seventy-one, he rocked. When he launched
into "All My Loving," a number he'd sung in Milwaukee with the
Beatles all those years ago, I couldn't help myself. I screamed.

3

Justin Vernon

The Journey to Bon Iver

Great artists have been known to disappear into the wilderness and return with masterpieces, most famously Henry David Thoreau with *Walden*. Justin Vernon followed this path with the Bon Iver album *For Emma, Forever Ago*, which imbues the solitary-genius genre with a Wisconsin chill.

In 2006, Vernon was a twenty-five-year-old Eau Claire native living in North Carolina when the bottom fell out. His band broke up, as did his romantic relationship, and these disappointments were followed by a health scare. He returned to Wisconsin to spend the winter alone in a remote Dunn County hunting cabin and reset his spirit. But what began as an aimless hibernation—watching hours of the TV series *Northern Exposure* while huddled up with a six-pack—transformed into an artistic breakthrough.

Vernon experimented with falsetto vocals and electronic processing, morphing sounds into fragmented lyrics. He tried to catch a mood by drawing on both his surroundings and his subconscious. The nine tracks that emerged from his cabin recording sessions evoked his melancholy state of mind, with lyrics that hint at heartbreak and harmonies that evoke the Up-North twilight at ten below.

Vernon initially self-released *For Emma, Forever Ago* under the name Bon Iver, which he'd adapted from *Northern Exposure*. Residents of the show's Alaskan town welcome the year's first snow by wishing each other "bon hiver," French for "good winter."

For Vernon, it had been a good winter indeed. The album that flowed from his private pain found its way to the indie label Jagjaguwar and connected with the public, earning rave reviews and blockbuster sales. Vernon ascended to indie-rock superstardom with A-list collaborations, TV appearances, international tours, and Grammy Awards. Bon Iver, which Vernon turned into a band, continued to hold the world's attention with a series of increasingly ambitious albums, including *Bon Iver, Bon Iver; 22, A Million;* and *I, I.*

Though Vernon made it big, he never got too big for Eau Claire, where he'd grown up, played high school football, and studied religion in college. It has remained his place of residence as well as his passion. After *For Emma, Forever Ago* hit the charts, he got a tattoo of Wisconsin on his chest with his favorite western counties outlined. He built a studio and hotel in Eau Claire, started a local music festival, and even used an accountant from nearby Osseo rather than a sharpie from the East or West Coast. At Bon Iver concerts, he makes a point of acknowledging his hometown, a spot he considers sacred.

Vernon's grounding in Eau Claire helps explain why he remains one of the most down-to-earth pop stars. He wears old T-shirts, often keeps a scraggly beard, and avoids the usual round of celebrity interviews. He considers music not a road to riches, but a means of discovering who he is.

And what he is, undoubtedly, has everything to do with western Wisconsin.

4

Elvis Presley

The Last Miracle

Elvis Presley's story has religious overtones. A poor boy with divine talent rises from obscurity to become a rock and roll god. As a true believer, I've made pilgrimages to the two major Elvis shrines in the South: his modest birthplace in Tupelo, Mississippi, and Graceland, his not-so-modest mansion in Memphis.

But Wisconsinites needn't go that far to worship Elvis. The state has a sacred site of its own in Madison—not as well known, but authentic nonetheless. At a busy intersection on the east side, a small stone marker bears Elvis's image. It stands on the spot where the King of Rock and Roll performed a miracle in the middle of the night on June 24, 1977.

Presley had just flown into Madison for a concert the next day, and he still wore his sparkly blue jumpsuit from an earlier show in Des Moines. On the way to a hotel, his limousine stopped at the fateful intersection: East Washington Avenue and Highway 51. He gazed to his right and saw two toughs beating up a teenager at a corner gas station.

Elvis flung open the car door. "I can't let this happen," he said, snapping into savior mode.[1] Over the strenuous objections of his bodyguard, he strode toward the attackers.

Now, our hero was overweight and ailing in the summer of 1977. But he did have a black belt in karate and a not-unwarranted faith in his power to alter the course of human affairs.

One can only imagine the attackers' thoughts as a large, sparkling man advanced on them, throwing karate kicks and shouting, "I'll take you on!" One can only imagine their shame when they realized Elvis Presley himself had caught them in a disgraceful act. They stopped mid-punch as the victim fled to safety.

Elvis shook hands with astonished bystanders, jumped back in his limousine, and vanished into the night. Police officers and newspaper reporters showed up later to make sense of the visitation.

The gas station rescue constituted the last miracle of Presley's life. He died less than two months later, worn out by drugs and despair. But Wisconsin still has the plaque on the corner of Madison's East Washington Avenue and Highway 51 to prove that he truly walked among us, performing wondrous feats.

I've stood there more than once, staring at the patch of ground where the gas station used to be. I swear that, even as traffic whizzes by, you can feel the sparkling man's presence.

5

The Chordettes

Bring Us a Dream

Were teenagers really more wholesome in the 1940s and '50s? The Chordettes make you believe it. College friends Janet Ertel, Alice Mae Buschmann Spielvogel, Dorothy Schwartz, and Jinny Osborn formed the vocal quartet in Sheboygan in 1946, donning party dresses, elbow-length white gloves, and shapely Donna Reed hairdos. The would-be pop stars chose their name at a time when most musical groups opted for earnest over edgy. Female bachelors were bachelorettes, and female drum majors were majorettes, so why wouldn't four women singing lush chords be the Chordettes?

The group performed around town, inspired by cheerful pop acts like the Andrews Sisters and the Boswell Sisters. Osborn's father loved barbershop quartets, so that style also proved influential. They made their breakthrough in 1949 with a first-place performance on Arthur Godfrey's talent show, leading to a contract with Cadence Records. Then came their first bid for pop immortality: 1954's "Mr. Sandman."

This two-minute gem stayed at number one for seven weeks, and for good reason. No song better represents the innocent side of the 1950s. With sweet barbershop harmonies, the Chordettes beg Mr. Sandman to "bring us a dream"—that is, a cute guy to call their own. They hope he has wavy hair and think it would be "peachy" to meet him right away. Yes, they really say "peachy"—and, apparently, mean it. No wonder the bobbysoxers down at the malt shop made "Mr. Sandman" their anthem.

The Chordettes achieved pop immortality in the 1950s, but by the time
this photo was taken around 1962, their particular brand of innocence had
gone out of style. UNIVERSITY OF WISCONSIN-MADISON ARCHIVES, MILLS
MUSIC LIBRARY

Coincidentally, Elvis Presley cut his first record in 1954, and
soon rowdy rock and roll transformed the music business. While
many old-fashioned vocal groups fell out of favor, the Chordettes
tried to keep up with the times.

In 1958, they made their second bid for lasting fame with a more
exuberant two-minute gem called "Lollipop." The rhythms were
bolder than those of "Mr. Sandman," the harmonies pricklier. Still,
no one would mistake the Chordettes for 1950s juvenile delinquents.
"Lollipop" is about as clean-cut as rock and roll ever got. In live performances of the new hit, they smiled graciously and threw candy
to the audience.

The Chordettes continued to top the charts at the dawn of the
1960s, but their days were numbered. Bob Dylan and the Beatles
would soon change our view of Top 40 music, just as the feminist
movement would transform mainstream attitudes about women.
After one last tribute to puppy love called "Never on Sunday," Sheboygan's pop sensation broke up in 1964.

I don't think I'd want to live in the rainbow-colored fantasyland conjured up by "Mr. Sandman," "Lollipop," and the Chordettes' dozen other hits. But for two minutes at a time, it's an irresistible place to visit.

6

Nirvana and Butch Vig

An Artful Brutality

I slow down whenever I drive along the 1200 block of Madison's East Washington Avenue, staring at a brick building I've seen hundreds of times before. You'd never guess that one of rock's most remarkable albums got its start behind that unremarkable façade: Nirvana's *Nevermind*.

The two-story structure housed Smart Studios, founded in the 1980s to record local bands. Around 1989, its proto-grunge album *Twelve Point Buck,* by the nose-thumbing noise merchants Killdozer, caught the ear of little-known Seattle trio Nirvana. They liked the heavy sound and worked out a plan to record in the studio with owner-producer Butch Vig, a Viroqua native who later hit the bigtime with his own band, Garbage.

Nirvana arrived in Madison in April 1990 with a bunch of half-finished numbers. Vig immediately recognized the potential in leader Kurt Cobain's songwriting and tortured vocals. He also saw that the tortured part was no put-on. Cobain often sank into dark moods, sitting by himself in a corner of the studio. Sometimes he sang so ferociously that he burned out after a take or two. "I'm not gonna crack," he wailed on "Lithium," though clearly he was getting close.

At the mixing board, Vig made magic with Cobain's primal screams. He turned them into accessible pop music without sacrificing a bit of their potency. The producer and the band finished *Nevermind* in Los Angeles, using the Smart Studios tracks as a template. One recording from the Madison sessions, "Polly," did end up on the album with no further tinkering—a pure dose of

Kurt's moodiness. You can imagine him mumbling the lyrics about "dirty wings" to himself in his private corner of the studio.

Nevermind hit number one in 1992, an astounding achievement for this angry album. I was among those who recognized themselves in songs like "Smells Like Teen Spirit" and "Breed"—four-minute outbursts of confusion and pain. I'd heard high-decibel angst before, in 1970s and '80s punk, but Nirvana achieved a more artful brutality thanks to Cobain's singing and lyrics. A whole generation was inspired by this out-of-control character who gained masterful control in his music.

Outside of music, the crackup continued. Nirvana fell silent after Cobain's suicide in 1994. Smart Studios closed in 2010, and the building is now just another faded storefront on East Washington Avenue. Whenever I drive by, though, "Smells Like Teen Spirit" cranks up one more time, at least inside my head.

7

Liberace

Mr. Showmanship

Wisconsin has a certain reputation in pop culture. America's Dairyland. Boring and bland. But if that's true, how do you explain Liberace?

Walter Liberace came from a devout Catholic family in West Allis, where he mesmerized friends and neighbors as an elementary-school piano prodigy in the 1920s. After a residency at Wausau's Wunderbar, where he used the stage name Walter Busterkeys, the twenty-year-old played a brilliant concerto with the Chicago Symphony Orchestra at Milwaukee's Pabst Theater. But he soon lost interest in a straight classical-music career. Mr. Busterkeys had a taste for razzle-dazzle.

In the 1940s, he dropped the name Walter and billed himself simply as Liberace. His flashy new act mixed virtuosic classical works with crowd-pleasing popular music. Audiences loved it, and Liberace got the message. Flashiness was his future.

From the 1950s until his death in 1987, Liberace earned the name Mr. Showmanship. He trafficked in excess, always delivered with a friendly wink. He was known to arrive onstage in a Rolls-Royce or suspended from a wire. His act featured showgirls and comedy routines, and he also perfected a literally splashy gimmick called the Dancing Waters, which involved geysers spouting onstage while he played a Strauss waltz.

Liberace treated audiences to ornately decorated pianos, topped with his trademark candelabra. His costumes included a beaded tuxedo, an ostrich-feather robe, and purple hotpants, not to mention a white llama-fur coat with a sixteen-foot train. He once told a

The pianist Liberace founded an act on flashiness, applied equally to Chopin and "Chopsticks." WHI IMAGE ID 59136

reporter, "I didn't come here to go unnoticed."[1] As for music, he gleefully mixed *Pagliacci* with "Home on the Range" and Chopin with "Chopsticks."

Classical purists dutifully scorned Liberace's flamboyant piano playing, but he couldn't have cared less. Flamboyance worked. He starred in a TV show, appeared in movies, commanded Las Vegas stages, and often made more per year than any other entertainer in the world. In response to criticism, he famously quipped, "I cried all the way to the bank."[2]

In an era when homophobia kept most gay celebrities confined to the closet, Liberace lived relatively openly. He never declared his sexual orientation, but he hinted at it every night onstage—a liberating gesture for his gay fans.

Tell-all books and movies have tried to strip off Liberace's glorious façade, but what's the use of that? Without his glorious façade, the twentieth century would have been considerably less fun.

8

Bob Dylan

Wow Wow Toaster

Singer, songwriter, Nobel Prize laureate, and oracle, Bob Dylan stands with the greatest American artists. And believe it or not, his path to immortality passed through a few shabby student apartments at the University of Wisconsin.

In January 1961, the nineteen-year-old University of Minnesota dropout headed to Madison with his acoustic guitar and harmonica, hoping to conquer the campus folk scene. He managed to meet the top UW folkies but, alas, did not impress them. At that point, only Dylan saw himself as a musical genius. He performed for students at Groves Women's Cooperative, whined Woody Guthrie songs at a few campus parties, and turned precisely zero heads. What most people noticed was the kid's oddball outfit: a brown suit and a skinny tie.

How did it feel to be in Madison as a complete unknown, with no direction home? "I've been broke and cold," he wrote to friends back in Minneapolis.[1] The future looked grim.

Dylan crashed with his new UW acquaintances for about a week and a half—and then fate intervened. A roommate offered him a ride to New York City, folk music's mecca. The determined teenager jumped at the offer, arrived in Greenwich Village, and started the artistic transformation that would soon lead to "Blowin' in the Wind," "A Hard Rain's A-Gonna Fall," and superstardom. When he traveled to Madison again in May 1961, staying with friends for another couple weeks, his guitar and vocals rang with new authority.

That same year, Dylan wrote the lyrics to a song-in-progress on a sheet of paper. It began, "Wisconsin is the dairy state / I guess you all know well / I was in Wow Wow Toaster there / The truth to you I'll tell."[2] Wisconsin residents will recognize that "Wow Wow Toaster" is Wauwatosa, which the song's narrator calls home. He also gushes that Madison and Milwaukee set his "heart aglow."

Indeed, the song bursts with love for all things Wisconsin. The speaker dreams of feasting on the state's milk and cream. He imagines strumming his banjo and twiddling his mustache amid the beautiful hills. Dylan never recorded the piece, and no music survives, so it's hard to judge the tone. He's undoubtedly poking fun at the state, but I think he's also expressing real affection. He did, after all, attend Jewish summer camp in the northern village of Webster during adolescence, and he also regularly visited relatives in Superior.

Wisconsin's official state song, "On, Wisconsin," dates from 1913 and reflects a stuffier era. "On, Wisconsin! On, Wisconsin! / Grand old Badger State! / We, thy loyal sons and daughters, / Hail thee, good and great!"

I, for one, am glad Dylan's ode exists as a more playful alternative. You can have thy grand old Badger State—bury my heart in Wow Wow Toaster.

9

Bunny Berigan

Pouring His Heart Out

Bernard "Bunny" Berigan was a Swing Era musician who made several fine recordings along with a truly fabulous one. It's the fabulous one—a 1937 interpretation of Vernon Duke and Ira Gershwin's "I Can't Get Started"—that justifies a state historical marker in his hometown of Fox Lake.

The marker informs passersby that Bunny got his start playing jazz trumpet in Beaver Dam and Madison, went on to perform with famous musicians like Benny Goodman and Bing Crosby, and led his own orchestra. It mentions "I Can't Get Started" only in passing, calling it "his most popular hit." But "I Can't Get Started" is more than just a hit. It's one of the most emotional outpourings in American music: a cry from the heart that endures long after most songs from the 1930s have faded.

I can attest to this recording's power, as it touched me at age thirteen. I was a child of 1970s pop rather than Swing Era jazz, but I stumbled across "I Can't Get Started" on a big-band compilation record. The trumpet grabbed me in the first bar—a soulful ascending phrase that practically says, "Sit down, I have a story to tell you." Throughout the opening cadenza, Bunny's horn pleads and implores, the sound of a man confessing his secrets to anyone who'll listen.

After a pregnant pause, the trumpeter states the melody of "I Can't Get Started," with drippy orchestral accompaniment. The corny arrangement, plus Berigan's simpering vocal, remind you that this is indeed a recording from a bygone era. But there's nothing corny about the climactic trumpet solo. Berigan wails, growls, and anguishes in every register of the horn. His majestic phrases transcend self-pity, suggesting a man's ability to keep his bearings in the midst of despair.

Throughout my troubled teens, I dropped the needle on "I Can't Get Started" over and over, until the record finally scratched. Later, I sought out information about the mysterious Bunny Berigan, whom I'd known only as a name on a track listing. Having memorized his tormented solo on "I Can't Get Started," I was not surprised to learn that the trumpeter hit rock bottom in the early 1940s. He flopped as an orchestra leader, went bankrupt, and drank himself to death at thirty-three. He's buried back in Fox Lake, where he'd first gained notice as a child prodigy.

Despite the handful of other gems in his brief career, Berigan made his claim on posterity with "I Can't Get Started," now enshrined in the Grammy Hall of Fame. For that alone, he deserves the historical marker in his hometown. Maybe even a museum.

10

Richard Davis

From a Broom to a Bass

No one considers Wisconsin the jazz capital of the world, but for many years it did have one thing New York City didn't: Richard Davis, bass player extraordinaire. Davis moved to the Madison area in the 1970s, when the University of Wisconsin–Madison lured him away from full-time performing in the Big Apple. Instantaneously, the city transformed into a global hot spot for jazz bass.

Davis grew up in Chicago in the 1930s, strumming on a broom before he could afford his first instrument. Trips to downtown music shops turned up recordings by Louis Armstrong and Duke Ellington, which he savored and studied. When Ellington's "Ko Ko" came on, the boy put his ear up to the speaker to hear bassist Jimmy Blanton's artfully timed breaks. These self-directed listening sessions set him on his zigzagging musical path.

Davis hit the bigtime in 1957 as a member of vocalist Sarah Vaughan's mainstream jazz combo. On her album *Swingin' Easy*, his supple walking bass propelled classic versions of "All of Me," "Pennies from Heaven," and "Body and Soul." Next, he switched from classic to confrontational on saxophonist Eric Dolphy's 1964 avant-garde album *Out to Lunch*. Bassists don't usually push themselves to the front of a jazz combo, but this one made his presence known with booming double stops, expressive glissandos, and soulful bowing.

Out to Lunch scrambled my synapses in high school, and after noting Davis's name on the album jacket, I started seeing it everywhere. There he was setting the mood on Van Morrison's melancholy *Astral Weeks*. There he was laying down suave rhythms behind

The adventurous bassist Richard Davis, pictured around 1989, was never content to be a mere accompanist. UNIVERSITY OF WISCONSIN–MADISON ARCHIVES, PHOTO BY BRENT NICASTRO

Frank Sinatra and Barbra Streisand. He even turned up in classical settings under Leonard Bernstein's baton.

When I moved to Madison, I couldn't believe my luck to find Davis as a UW faculty member who played around town, from concert halls to corner bars. A thousand miles away from New York City, I felt like I'd landed in jazz heaven. He was by turns earthy and elegant, melding gutbucket moans with graceful pizzicato. His bass was not just a solid foundation: it was the fire in the furnace. With his fluid time and varied attack, he made every chorus an adventure.

Once, I traveled to Manhattan to see Davis in his natural habit, leading an all-star quintet at the Village Vanguard. He served as both accompanist and commander in chief, forging the band's sound while also graciously stepping aside to let the other musicians shine. He helped each soloist create a full-blown dramatic statement, choking the time or letting it breathe. He'd build momentum, reach a series of mini-climaxes, and then back off. When the big climaxes finally came, they felt earned—and were often overwhelming.

A framed picture of Davis hung on the club's wall near one of his boyhood idol Louis Armstrong, marking the distance he had traveled from his broom-strumming days.

After the show, Davis greeted fans, including a woman who asked him for directions to Madison. It seemed an odd request in the middle of Manhattan but not completely out of left field. Of course a music lover would need directions to Madison, given that Davis had made it the jazz bass capital of the world.

11

Buddy Holly

A Sure Cure for Gloominess

Buddy Holly's death is associated with Clear Lake, Iowa, where he headlined his final rock and roll show on February 2, 1959. To make his next date, Holly took the then-unusual step of chartering a small plane for himself and his tour mates Ritchie Valens and the Big Bopper. The plane went down in a snowstorm and killed all three, a tragedy known as The Day the Music Died. Though the crash site is in Iowa, Wisconsin plays a role in this sad story.

The Clear Lake date was part of a tour called the Winter Dance Party, which had started ten days earlier in Milwaukee's Million Dollar Ballroom, then proceeded to Kenosha, Eau Claire, and Green Bay, among other cities in Iowa and Minnesota. A callous booking agent had scheduled the dates haphazardly. In blizzard conditions, the musicians traveled hundreds of miles between one-night stands on a rundown bus. The bus died on the way to Appleton and stranded them on a deserted highway near Hurley in negative thirty–degree temps. To stay warm, they set fire to newspapers in the aisle.

A couple days later, on the road from Green Bay to Clear Lake, Holly had his brainstorm. He would charter a plane for a hassle-free trip to the next gig. That would give him a chance to do his laundry and get some rest.

Every February, I fantasize about seeing one of Buddy's last shows in Wisconsin. He played "Peggy Sue," "That'll Be the Day," and other irrepressible hits that set the style for early rock and roll. No matter how hopeless I feel when contemplating Holly's shortened career, I can't help but smile at his profoundly hopeful music.

With his elastic vocals and ecstatic guitar, he embodied the youthful spirit that upended the record industry in the late 1950s.

I also fantasize about meeting Buddy after one of these shows. Back then, rock stars didn't hide behind security details. Holly pulled up a chair and greeted his Wisconsin fans. I imagine telling him how happy his songs make me feel, then offering to drive him to the next date so he won't have to travel on an unreliable bus. Or plane.

Of course, I can only fantasize for so long until reality sets in, like the Wisconsin chill. Buddy did charter that plane. He died at twenty-two, never knowing he would influence the Beatles, Bob Dylan, the Rolling Stones, and countless others, changing the course of music history. Gloom overtakes me once again.

Luckily, there's a sure cure for gloominess in this world. It's Buddy Holly's music.

12

Duke Ellington

A Polka for Wisconsin

It's hard to imagine Duke Ellington as neglected. Decades after his death in 1974, we take him for granted as a homegrown genius: the composer and pianist who moved the jazz orchestra from dance music to art music beginning in the 1920s. His swinging tone poems proved that earthy sounds such as growling trombones and wailing saxophones could figure into a grand artistic vision. "Mood Indigo," "(In My) Solitude," and "It Don't Mean a Thing (If It Ain't Got That Swing)" are staples of the great American songbook.

But the cultural gatekeepers in Ellington's heyday did not see jazz as art. They considered it too coarse to be important, no matter how much it mattered to audiences or to hip music critics. Duke would receive no Pulitzer Prize for Music in the 1940s, when he balanced compositional rigor with spontaneous expression in "Ko-Ko" and "Concerto for Cootie." And in the days before the National Endowment for the Arts, he would receive no government support when his band fell on hard times in the 1950s. Instead, he was forced to play background music at an ice show.

Ellington also suffered the same humiliations as other Black Americans of his time. Jim Crow laws forced Black musicians to avoid white-only hotels, restrooms, and restaurants. They generally couldn't even walk through a venue's front doors or sit at tables near white patrons. Ellington grew accustomed to such slights, including a racially tinged rejection for a Pulitzer Prize in 1965. The Pulitzer jury recommended him for a special citation, but the board refused to grant it to a mere jazz musician. "Fate is being kind to

Jazz master Duke Ellington in 1973, just after his career-capping experience in Wisconsin. WIKIMEDIA COMMONS

me," the sixty-six-year-old composer bitterly joked in response to the snub. "Fate doesn't want me to be famous too young."[1]

In 1972, however, the University of Wisconsin–Madison made an uncommon gesture for the era, granting Ellington an honorary doctorate and mounting a weeklong festival of his music. Duke and his band members had the rare chance to conduct master classes, and Governor Patrick Lucey announced "Duke Ellington Week" throughout the state. Ellington considered it one of his greatest honors.

In response, he proclaimed his love for Wisconsin, from the beer to the cheese to the people. He also expressed his gratitude in a suite written for the occasion, called "UWIS"—a bluesy, harmonically rich portrait of the state. An innovator to the end, Ellington took the opportunity to experiment with jazz form, even scoring his first polka. That section delighted the polka-loving Wisconsin crowd when the orchestra performed "UWIS" at a July 21 concert.

Ellington created the piece, he said, "to evoke some of the happiness that Wisconsin and the inhabitants of that state had given me."[2] Now there's something Wisconsin can be proud of: making Duke Ellington happy.

13

Woody Herman

Blue Flame

I don't know what inspired me to buy *Woody Herman's Greatest Hits* at age twelve. The record was cheap—only ninety-nine cents in the store's bargain bin—and the name "Woody" probably seemed fun, like the cartoon character Woody Woodpecker. But whatever the reason, it's one of the luckiest things I ever did. That album of big-band jazz ushered me into an alternate universe of harmony, melody, and rhythm, and I never wanted to leave.

Born in Milwaukee in 1913, Herman inherited a love of music from his showbiz parents and got started early on reed instruments. He joined a vaudeville act as "The Boy Wonder of the Clarinet," then played in a local bar band. He made his first record at sixteen and studied at the Marquette University School of Music for a year. After that, he left Wisconsin for a new home: the road.

Herman formed his own swing orchestra at twenty-three, scoring a hit with 1939's bluesy "Woodchopper's Ball." But commercial success mattered less to him than following his muse—indeed, the group was once dismissed from a Chicago ballroom for playing "too loud and too fast."[1] He had an ear for new sounds and began incorporating the subversive bebop style into his big-band numbers. In the 1940s, his madcap band of young musicians, dubbed the Herd, shook up the musical establishment with a series of recordings that rank among jazz's finest—and, often, funniest.

These were the tracks on my greatest-hits album. Every time I hear "Blue Flame," the band's theme song, the ominous mood puts me on edge. The trombones lay down haunting half notes while

Herman slithers up a blues scale on clarinet. A corresponding chill always runs up my spine.

The Herd excelled at such atmospheric music but made its international breakthrough with livelier fare like "Apple Honey" and "Wild Root." Raucous and irreverent, such recordings sound as fresh today as they did in the '40s. On "Caldonia," Herman sings nonsense lyrics while his bandmates chime in with startling screams. On "Northwest Passage," the ensemble tosses off casually virtuosic passages at a supercharged tempo as if it were the easiest thing in the world. (As a big-band veteran myself, I can report: it isn't.) "Four Brothers" embodies jazz's essential dialectic, skillfully balancing spontaneity and control.

Herman led various incarnations of the Herd until the end of his life in 1987—no mean feat given the decline of big-band jazz in the 1950s. True to form, he continued to experiment with new sounds. His orchestra premiered "Ebony Concerto," an avant-garde work by Igor Stravinsky, and plugged in during the Woodstock era with an arrangement of the Doors' "Light My Fire."

When I saw the Herd in Madison, shortly before Herman's death, his blue flame still burned brightly. He was no longer a boy, but he remained a wonder.

14

Otis Redding

Loving by the Pound

Otis Redding had a brief and tragic moment in Wisconsin. In 1967, the twenty-six-year-old rhythm and blues singer died in Madison's Lake Monona when his plane crashed en route to a concert in terrible weather.

Madison did not take this twist of fate lightly. The city built a monument to Redding on the lakeshore, and local media regularly retell the story of his crash on December 10.

As a Madison resident, I've preserved the singer's memory in my own way. When my son was born, I wanted to cultivate a feeling for music. None of my child-rearing books covered this topic, so I had to improvise. The solution I hit on was Otis Redding. I decided to play Redding's songs for my newborn every day for the first year. If that didn't hardwire music into a baby's brain, nothing would. I began a steady diet of hits like "Respect" and "(Sittin' On) The Dock of the Bay," though our favorite was the lesser-known "Loving by the Pound." We both giggled and squealed while twirling around the room.

Can an early dose of Otis Redding really teach a child to appreciate music? I can't speak to its scientific validity but will say that my homemade experiment worked. Even in elementary school, Jo responded to soulful sounds in a wide range of styles, from jazz to hip-hop to classical music, then formed a band with two fifth-grade neighbors. I give all credit to Otis.

When Jo grew old enough, however, I faced a difficult task. I had to explain the story of Redding's life, complete with its sad ending in our hometown. Otis came out of Georgia in the late 1950s and recorded his first single with the Stax label at age twenty-one. He moved audiences around the world with his raw performances, singing about love more viscerally than any pop star of the day. Indeed, he made his most lasting impression during 1967's Summer of Love at the Monterey International Pop Festival. A half year later, he went ahead with his flight to Madison despite dangerous rain and fog. He didn't want to let down his local fans.

But I try not to think too much about what happened on December 10, 1967. When it comes to Otis Redding, I try to think about love. Loving by the pound.

15

Frank Morgan

Redemption and Rebirth

As a seven-year-old Milwaukee kid, Frank Morgan was already a pretty good guitarist, following in the footsteps of his father, a professional musician. But in 1940, his dad took him to a show featuring alto saxophonist Charlie Parker, an acquaintance who was about to revolutionize jazz with the modernist style called bebop. The experience changed Morgan's life—for better and for worse.

The minute he heard Parker's starkly beautiful sound, he knew that alto sax was his destiny. His dad introduced the two backstage, and Parker showed an interest in the boy. The next day, he took young Frank to a music store and helped him pick out a reed instrument. Before long, Frank was Parker's protégé, copying the master's quirky melodies and quicksilver rhythms.

At fourteen, the whiz kid sat in with top jazz players in Los Angeles. And at twenty-two, when he released his debut album, word spread that he might be "the next Charlie Parker."

But before that could happen, Morgan succumbed to drug addiction, just as Parker had. His heroin habit led to a life of forgery and theft, and he spent most of the next thirty years behind bars. Instead of taking his place in the pantheon of jazz legends, as some had predicted, he performed solely for fellow inmates in the San Quentin prison band. "In prison, the instrument was what kept me sane," he later said, "and the chance to play it kept me with hope."[1]

After his release in 1985, Morgan finally recorded a second album, drawing on decades of pent-up emotion. Because prison had isolated him from a generation's worth of musical changes, listeners got the impression that an obscure 1950s bebop virtuoso had magically materialized in the 1980s.

Morgan's resurrection fascinated the public, and his friendly smile beamed out of magazines and TV screens. Audiences responded to his hot solos and warm manner. He expressed gratitude for his long-delayed fame and hoped to earn people's respect. "I really intend to play," he said, "and to play my heart out."[2]

That meant staying off drugs, which required herculean effort. To avoid temptation, Morgan dedicated himself to practicing and recording. He also moved back to Milwaukee in 1994 to live around supportive family members, who accompanied him on daily trips to a methadone clinic.

I interviewed Morgan after his return to Wisconsin, a state he dubbed "pretty hip."[3] He credited Milwaukee with giving him his start in music and the city's schools with providing him an excellent education. And he appreciated the kindness of local jazz fans.

I saw Morgan play a triumphant concert in Madison and followed his career until he died from cancer in 2007, at age seventy-three. His final years constituted one of the great second acts in jazz history, and his recordings endure as a testament to redemption and rebirth.

In our talk, Morgan explained his musical strategy of channeling everything he felt through his horn. He strove to make a direct connection between his heart and a listener's heart.

I'd say: mission accomplished.

16

Viola Smith

The Fastest Girl Drummer

With just a few hundred inhabitants, Mount Calvary managed to produce a jazz drummer of national significance. She was born back in 1912, but if you stop modern-day residents on the main drag, they still know her name: Viola Smith.

Viola's father owned a ballroom in the tiny village. On my visit in 2023, townsfolk showed me where it once stood on the 100 block of Fond du Lac Street. Mr. Smith needed entertainment, so he enlisted his five eldest daughters into a jazzy family orchestra: Irene on trombone, Loretta on piano, Edwina on trumpet, and Sally and Lila on sax. By the time thirteen-year-old Viola was ready to join the band, they still needed a drummer. She stomped on the high hat, smacked the snare, and fell in love with bangs and booms.

The Smith sisters expanded to an octet with two more siblings, hitting the road as a rare all-female orchestra at Wisconsin fairs and vaudeville theaters. Viola closely watched other drummers on the circuit and asked them for advice. They passed on what they knew about paradiddles and flams, and the precocious teenager developed her own flashy way of playing.

One by one, the Smith sisters left music for other pursuits. But not Viola. Since most orchestras were closed to female instrumentalists, she formed a women's jazz band called the Coquettes in 1939 to showcase her showy style. Her twelve-piece kit sat on a tall platform, with two giant tom-toms at shoulder height—an innovation that wowed the crowds when Viola rapped out rhythms at full speed. To end the numbers with a flourish, she bounced her sticks off a drumhead and caught them in midair.

Viola Smith (far left) smacked her snare drum in the 1920s with Wisconsin's Schmitz (later Smith) Sisters Orchestra, the forerunner of her nationally celebrated all-woman jazz band, the Coquettes. UNIVERSITY OF WISCONSIN–MADISON ARCHIVES, MILLS MUSIC LIBRARY

The odds were stacked against women in jazz, but the Coquettes impressed the music industry with their percussive thunder. Smith became a phenom, earning the nickname "The Fastest Girl Drummer in the World." She befriended top male drummers Gene Krupa, Jo Jones, and Buddy Rich, and in 1940, *Billboard* magazine splashed her image on its cover, mallets blazing.

In 1942, as men left jazz bands to fight in World War II, Smith saw an opportunity for women players. She wrote an impassioned article for *Down Beat* magazine called "Give Girl Musicians a Break!," urging bandleaders to hire these overlooked instrumentalists. "Why not let the girls play in the big-name bands?" she asked. "They are as much the masters of their instruments as are male musicians."[1] The article proved influential and opened doors for Smith, Melba Liston, Billie Rogers, and other great players who yearned to show their stuff.

Smith performed with jazz luminaries Ella Fitzgerald and Chick Webb, starred with the popular Hour of Charm Orchestra, then toured as a solo act with a spectacular seventeen-piece drum kit in the 1950s. She even studied classical music at the Juilliard School and joined the National Symphony Orchestra as a timpanist. In 2000, Lincoln Center for the Performing Arts rightly honored her as a jazz legend.

Viola Smith continued to sock her cymbals and slam her snare drum beyond the age of one hundred, defying the conventional view of elderly women as past their prime. She died at 107 in 2020, a hero to generations of female instrumentalists who followed her lead in the music business. The most common word in the major-media obituaries was *trailblazing.*

It's no wonder people still know her name in Mount Calvary. Who could forget The Fastest Girl Drummer in the World?

17

Grafton Blues Musicians

Love, Sex, Death

In the middle of 1931's "22-20 Blues," Mississippi bluesman Skip James sings an unexpected word: "Wisconsin." As the speaker fantasizes about killing his "unruly" lover, James wails, "All the doctors in Wisconsin, they won't help her none!" Why would a musician from the Deep South refer to Wisconsin, of all places? It turns out that James was sitting in a Grafton recording studio as he sang that line, probably thinking it up on the spot.

In 1917, the Wisconsin Chair Company made the unlikely decision to start a music business on the side. The furniture maker already sold phonograph cabinets and figured it could cash in on the new craze for records. The company created several labels, mostly featuring country bands and regional orchestras few people care about anymore. But its Paramount label shrewdly recorded several Southern blues artists who, though obscure at the time, now rank as giants of American music.

We might not know the names Skip James, Charley Patton, Son House, Geeshie Wiley, or Elvie Thomas if they hadn't made the long trip north to Grafton, where the Wisconsin Chair Company built its barnlike recording studio. They sat in a cold, damp room, whose walls were covered with blankets to reduce the reverberation, and sang into an eight-foot-long wooden horn that led to a primitive microphone. Picking their battered acoustic guitars or pounding on the studio's upright piano, they sang nakedly emotional numbers about life's elemental experiences: love, sex, death. Patton's "Pony Blues," House's "Preaching the Blues," and Wiley and Thomas's

"Motherless Child Blues" cast a spell on generations of blues, folk, and rock artists.

In other words, Grafton played a significant part in music history. If you don't believe me, just listen to the many cover versions of James's "22-20 Blues." You'll hear everybody from Robert Johnson to Eric Clapton to the Cowboy Junkies sing the word "Wisconsin."

In today's Grafton, you find historical markers about the legendary musicians but no recording studio. Paramount stopped making records in 1932, a result of declining sales during the Great Depression and its own unscrupulous business practices. Paramount workers, resentful about losing their jobs, reportedly took records from the warehouse and threw them into the nearby Milwaukee River. Area residents used others to patch holes in their walls, and the factory burned the rest for fuel.

Nobody knows exactly what went missing in the aftermath. Did Paramount attract other Southern greats we never got to hear—piano players, guitar strummers, and harmonica blowers who journeyed to Grafton for a few dollars per side?

It's enough to make you want to rent a scuba suit, dive into the Milwaukee River, and search for sunken treasure.

18

Les Paul
The Wizard of Waukesha

Les Paul is arguably Wisconsin's most influential musician. He pioneered the solid-body electric guitar, multitrack recording, close-miking, and other innovations that transformed the music industry. And his effects-heavy guitar playing enchanted generations of jazz, rock, and country artists. These accomplishments earned him a nickname that was both dazzling and down-home: "The Wizard of Waukesha."

Paul was born in Waukesha in 1915, the redheaded son of an auto mechanic. He started performing locally at twelve, billing himself as Red Hot Red. He never learned to read music but developed a swinging guitar style that impressed regional jazz and country bands. When he dropped out of high school to go on the road, however, few would have guessed at the wonders to come.

In his spare time, Les tinkered with inventions, using the materials he had at hand. His first experiments with amplifying a guitar involved a railroad tie and two spikes. Later, he created a solid-body electric guitar from a block of wood, calling it The Log. This presaged the Les Paul guitar, introduced by Gibson in 1952 and revered to this day.

Paul made it to the top of the pops backing Bing Crosby and the Andrews Sisters. In the 1940s, he created an eccentric hit recording of his own called "Lover," which overwhelmed the ear with eight overdubbed guitars. The homemade technological trick turned a one-man band into an orchestra.

Paul perfected the overdubbing technique on a series of irresistible top-ten songs with singer Mary Ford. The two married in

Les Paul, a.k.a. Red Hot Red, became obsessed with amplifying his guitar in the 1920s. PHOTO COURTESY OF WAUKESHA COUNTY HISTORICAL SOCIETY & MUSEUM

Milwaukee and became a showbiz sensation in the 1950s with their radio and TV shows. Their versions of standards like "Tiger Rag," "I'm Sitting on Top of the World," and "How High the Moon" layered Mary's multitracked voice with Les's bright guitar. Listening to "Tiger Rag" without smiling is, quite simply, impossible—not with Ford purring "Here kitty kitty kitty" while Paul's guitar provides meowing glissandos.

But after this heady success came a setback. Arthritis, hearing loss, and a hand injury forced Paul out of the music business in the 1960s.

The story might have ended there, but the Wizard of Waukesha had a few miracles left in him. In the 1970s and '80s, he revamped his playing style to accommodate his physical limitations and made a Grammy-winning comeback. In 1983, he launched weekly residencies in Manhattan jazz clubs that lasted almost to his death in 2009, at ninety-four. Admirers such as Paul McCartney, Keith Richards, and Jimmy Buffett dropped by to pay their respects.

In his final years, Les Paul received the sort of acclaim that most artists only dream about. The Rock and Roll Hall of Fame and the Smithsonian Institution honored him with exhibitions, and he took his rightful place in the National Inventors Hall of Fame. Shortly before his death, he returned to Waukesha to raise funds for a permanent Les Paul exhibition at the Waukesha County Museum. *Les Paul's House of Sound*, a display at Milwaukee's Discovery World, also enshrines him as a local legend.

These are stunning achievements for a high school dropout who never learned to read music. But of course you'd expect nothing less from a wizard.

19

Roscoe Mitchell

A Virtuoso of the Unexpected

In its heyday, the Art Ensemble of Chicago filled a stage with instruments not usually seen in jazz: bassoons, conch shells, whistles, glockenspiels, sirens, gourds. Three of the quintet's members walked out in African face paint, beads, and robes, and one in a white lab coat. Saxophonist Roscoe Mitchell, the member based in Wisconsin, wore street clothes. The show might begin with a moment of silence, followed by a dreamlike improvisation on gongs, chimes, congas, and bells.

After that, anything could happen. The cloud of percussion morphed into a bebop riff, a polka interlude, a bugle call, a reggae rhythm, a chorus of high-pitched bird calls, or an unaccompanied tenor solo by Mitchell. With no preset harmony, melody, or tempo to guide their improvisation, the musicians relied on reflexes to hold things together.

Mitchell, Lester Bowie, Malachi Favors, Joseph Jarman, and Don Moye were virtuosos of the unexpected. They played not jazz but what they called "Great Black Music—Ancient to the Future," embracing African chants, spirituals, rhythm and blues, and rock and roll. With its ceaselessly shifting textures and moods, their music was equal parts chaos and control. Mitchell attributed its power to "the unknown."[1]

Roscoe Mitchell grew up in Chicago and in 1965 helped found the city's Association for the Advancement of Creative Musicians, whose members helped each other expand the frontiers of improvised music. The Art Ensemble of Chicago emerged from this utopian scene: a leaderless group of individuals contributing equally to what Mitchell called "a total sound image."

The group struggled for recognition and resources in the 1960s and early '70s, but Mitchell never considered stepping off his experimental path. "You'd have to give up your opportunity to explore what you feel and what you hear," he told me, "and that's the reason I'm in music."

Free-jazz lovers eventually responded to their charismatic live performances and idiosyncratic albums. In 1979, the Art Ensemble of Chicago signed with the popular ECM label for a record called *Nice Guys* (an ironic comment on their reputation as noisy hell-raisers), which kicked off an era of widespread acclaim. They won critics' polls and became avant-garde idols.

The group's egalitarianism allowed the five strong personalities to stay together for decades. Simultaneously, Mitchell maintained a solo career from his home base in Wisconsin—first Hollandale, then Madison and Fitchburg. As he did with the Art Ensemble of Chicago, he kept audiences guessing at his local shows. I once saw him sustain a note for five minutes via circular breathing. With his reed barely vibrating, he invited listeners to savor the distinction between sibilance and silence. I often watched him plunge into brave new worlds of space and sound, bending time like a possessed shaman. Such musical heroics earned him a 2020 Jazz Masters Fellowship from the National Endowment for the Arts.

Appreciating Mitchell's performances requires a listener to tolerate new standards of beauty and, as Mitchell does himself, to embrace the unknown.

"There's readings that say that a long time ago, musicians were so highly developed that they were able to sit around in these robes, and they'd cover themselves and disappear," he said. "I've never done that, but it's nice to think about it—that it could happen. That's the level you'd be striving for."

To my knowledge, Mitchell has yet to disappear on stage. But I have no doubt he'll keep trying, night after thrilling night.

20

Little Richard

The Performer and the Penitent

I could have filled the Melody Makers section of this book with famous musicians who've played one-night stands in Wisconsin, from Enrico Caruso (1907) to Ella Fitzgerald (1959) to Bruce Springsteen (2023). But that would be cheating, given my stated goal of featuring only heroes who had a significant experience in the state. A one-night stand doesn't usually rise to that level. However amazing an evening's performance in Wisconsin may be, a musician often replicates it the next night in Minnesota, Illinois, or Michigan.

I will make an exception, however, for Little Richard's show at the Wisconsin State Fair in West Allis on August 8, 1996. It struck a blow for freedom that resonates to this day, at least in my family.

Richard Penniman was born in Macon, Georgia, in 1932, with one leg shorter than the other. His disability, along with being gay in repressive times, led to bullying by his religious community and even his own father. He agonized between trying to fit in and expressing his true nature, including his wild style of singing and playing piano.

When Penniman decided to let it all hang out as "Little Richard" in the mid-1950s, the world shifted on its axis. His lusty wails on "Tutti Frutti" and "Long Tall Sally" announced the birth of rock and roll and liberated an entire generation. Young listeners of the day, such as Elton John, David Bowie, Etta James, Tina Turner, Mick Jagger, John Lennon, and Paul McCartney, heard these ecstatic outbursts and found the courage to express their own true natures.

Fast forward to West Allis in 1996. Entering the state fairgrounds, I expected not only a concert but also a kind of psycho-
drama. At age sixty-four, Little Richard still agonized over his
identity. Multiple times in his career, he had renounced rock and
roll in favor of gospel music. In terms of his own mental health, the
price of rock and roll—this gift he gave to all of us—was steep. Who
would he be at this show: the performer or the penitent?

I took a seat at the outdoor venue with my wife, eight months
pregnant with our first child. Watching openers Mitch Ryder and
Jerry Lee Lewis proved excruciating due to the overzealous security guards. Anytime a fan so much as stood up to clap, sway, or sing
along—a perfectly natural response to "Devil with a Blue Dress
On" and "Great Balls of Fire"—the guards rushed over to enforce a
strict stay-in-your-seat policy that undermined the very idea of a
rock and roll show.

Penniman took the stage with big hair, big personality, and a big
blast of horns, allaying my fears of a Sunday school sermon. This
was Little Richard unbound, ready to "rip it up and ball tonight." He
introduced one of his saxophonists, a Milwaukee native, and spent
several minutes impressing upon us the awesomeness of a Wis-
consinite playing for fellow Wisconsinites on home turf. As a
Southerner with Macon deep in his soul, he appreciated the mysterious influence of a person's place of origin.

And then something extraordinary happened. Defying the
house rules, much as he had defied the rules of propriety in the 1950s,
Little Richard invited the whole crowd to join him on stage for a
sing-along. With a sidelong glance at the security guards, who knew
they'd been beaten, my pregnant wife and I made a beeline for Little
Richard's piano, along with hundreds of Wisconsin residents now
feeling the power and the glory of rock and roll freedom.

I have no idea what was happening in utero, but I can only imagine my unborn child absorbing an invaluable first lesson from those
joyous waves of sound.

Creators

21

Lynda Barry

A Nerd's-Eye View

In the 1980s, Lynda Barry made it safe to be a misfit. *Ernie Pook's Comeek*, her artfully crude comic strip for alternative weekly newspapers, evoked infinite varieties of dorkiness. Whether dramatizing romantic misadventures or childhood insecurities, Barry redeemed a generation of oddballs by finding the humor—and also the heartache—in our fails. In stories told from a nerd's-eye view, we recognized Barry as one of us.

Lynda was born in 1956 in Richland Center to an Irish-Norwegian father and an Irish-Filipino mother, and she spoke Tagalog at home. Around 1960, her unhappy family moved to Seattle, where her parents divorced and she suffered the poverty and neglect that would inspire a lifetime of art. When Barry entered Evergreen State College, the student newspaper editor Matt Groening (who would later create *The Simpsons*) announced a radical policy of printing anything contributors submitted. She tested the limits by turning in what she considered unprintable drawings, signed "Ernie Pook"—doodle-style images that appeared to be ripped from an impudent girl's notebook. Groening, bless him, stayed true to his word.

As luck would have it, the late 1970s was the heyday of alternative newsweeklies willing to publish previously unprintable work. *Ernie Pook's Comeek* found a home in dozens of counterculture newspapers around the country, including Madison's *Isthmus*, where I worked as an editor. Every week, staffers elbowed each other out of the way to get the first look at the comic when it arrived by mail. We pored over panels crammed with introspective text and childlike drawings, following the lives of geeky cousins Maybonne and Marlys.

One day, I stumbled across Barry—familiar from her redheaded self-caricature and quirky appearances on *Late Night with David Letterman*—wandering around the Capitol Square. She was on a cross-country jaunt to be chronicled in *Ernie Pook's Comeek*. I led her to the *Isthmus* office, where she endured our hero worship. Her trademark self-consciousness, so cringingly rendered in the comic, seemed true to life.

Over the next decades, Barry reached beyond her alt-weekly fan base with illustrated novels, a play, and how-to books about the creative process, such as *What It Is* and *Making Comics*. She also moved back to Wisconsin to settle in rural Footville and teach interdisciplinary creativity at the University of Wisconsin–Madison. Barry's idiosyncratic classes feature singing, dancing, joking, and hand-drawn syllabi. She assigns unconventional exercises, such as drawing with your eyes closed, and encourages students to use pseudonyms in class. Her own include Professor Hotdog, Professor Peanut, Professor Skeletor, and Hot Stuff the Little Devil.

There's a method to this delightful madness. Barry wants students to unleash their creativity by transcending adult inhibitions and thinking like children again. It's worked for her, and she knows it can work for almost anyone, from business majors to scientists. Listen to Professor Skeletor and find your inner genius.

And I don't use that word lightly. In 2019, Barry became the first cartoonist to win a prestigious MacArthur Fellowship "genius grant" for "inspiring creative engagement through original graphic works and a teaching practice centered on the role of image making in communication."[1]

Chalk one up for us misfits.

In her cartoons and classes, Lynda Barry, pictured at her desk in 2019, taps a wellspring of creativity by thinking like a child. © JOHN D. AND CATHERINE T. MACARTHUR FOUNDATION–USED WITH PERMISSION

22

The Ringling Brothers

A Grand Carnival of Fun

From our vantage point in the early twenty-first century, with cell phones in our pockets and streaming services on our TVs, it's difficult to imagine a United States starved for entertainment. So pity hardworking nineteenth-century Americans in the days before record players, movies, or even cars to drive to the nearest theatrical venue. If they lived in rural areas, as three-quarters of the population did in 1869, their best bet was to count down the days until a traveling circus came through town.

That year, Al, Otto, Charles, Alfred, and John Ringling got their first look at a circus in McGregor, Iowa, just across the Mississippi River from Prairie du Chien. A circus boat pulled into town and put on a shabby one-ring show with a cannonball-juggling strongman. But the event stirred up just enough pixie dust to entrance these sons of a humble McGregor harness maker. They fashioned their own tent from scraps of canvas, old carpets, and ratty army blankets and charged neighbors a penny each to watch their attempts at acrobatics and fancy horseback riding. This schoolboy production also featured a fat bullfrog that was purportedly "captured at great risk from a far-away swamp from which no other frog-collector ever emerged alive."[1] The bluster portended things to come.

Following the family's move to Baraboo, the five brothers conspired to lift themselves out of poverty by launching a professional circus. In 1882, the Ringling Brothers Classic and Comic Concert Company premiered in Mazomanie with a slate of music, comedy, dancing, and plate-spinning. That first show proved less than astonishing, due to their stage fright, but the Ringlings lacked the defeatist gene. With their meager profits, the boys bought top hats, evening suits, and a traveling wagon, renaming the show the Ringling Bros. Grand Carnival of Fun. "Grand" was a stretch, but it precisely defined where their ambitions lay.

Two more brothers joined the operation—Henry and Gus—along with a donkey and a Shetland pony. The Ringlings cut their tent poles from tamarack trees and upped the ante of their productions with a succession of new names over the years, such as the Ringling Bros. United Monster Shows, Great Double Circus, Royal European Menagerie, Museum, Caravan, and Congress of Trained Animals. They trudged along muddy roads to entertain small towns around the region, including Whitewater, Argyle, Elroy, Ironton, Stoughton, Poynette, Barron, Mount Horeb, Chippewa Falls, River Falls, Sauk City, and Boscobel. Their acts included "The Emperor of All Dutch Dialect Comedians" and "The Human Volcano," who bit off "bars of red hot iron, eating boiling and blazing sealing-wax."[2]

In typical American fashion, the Ringling brothers eternally aimed for the bigger and the better. More animals, more acrobats, more wagons, more thrills and chills, more patrons in ever-larger tents. In 1889, the brothers purchased eleven railroad cars and set out to conquer the nation from their headquarters in Baraboo. Incredibly, they did. The show's 1900 debut in Los Angeles caused a sensation, with the *Los Angeles Times* dubbing it "the circus of circuses."[3] The Ringlings bought up competing troupes, including Barnum & Bailey in 1907, and became the largest circus in the world. In other words, the Greatest Show on Earth.

They lived a century before the founding of People for the Ethical Treatment of Animals, and we now wince at the Ringlings' exploitation of elephants, bears, and tigers. In 2017, animal-rights protesters helped to temporarily shut down the operation, though at that point it had long since left Baraboo and no longer involved the Ringling family.

In their time, the Ringlings were known as upstanding citizens.

In 1905, Alfred, Charles, John, Al, and Otto Ringling were on the verge of creating "The Greatest Show on Earth." WHI IMAGE ID 6050

They succeeded through hard work, discipline, sound management, and good old-fashioned teamwork. This was a family that pulled together, with each member contributing a particular skill. Al, who'd begun as a juggler and tightrope walker, hired the acts. Charles produced the shows, Gus advertised them, and Alfred led the band. Otto handled the finances while John took care of transportation. Henry served as the advance man who mapped out parade routes.

In a golden age of grifters, the Ringling brothers earned a reputation for honesty and integrity. They tolerated no pickpockets or con artists on their grounds. They refused to shortchange customers or tear down competitors' posters. The press described them as "upright young men" and dubbed their circus a "Sunday School Show"—a testament to their strict Lutheran upbringing in Wisconsin.[4]

Most of all, the Ringlings deserve a tip of the top hat for bringing magic and mystery to the places that needed them most in the days before nickelodeons and Victrolas. Their advertisements guaranteed that "You will laugh as you never laughed before," in addition to promising "glorious art and dress in ravishing array."[5]

And they delivered on their promises. As one newspaper wrote of the Ringling brothers' 1889 show: "We conclude the public got all it paid for."[6]

23

Lorraine Hansberry

Through the Awful Hurt

Can you hang onto the American Dream while living an American nightmare? Lorraine Hansberry posed the question so memorably in 1959's *A Raisin in the Sun* that it became the first play by a Black woman to appear on Broadway, as well as the first by a Black playwright to win the New York Drama Critics' Circle Award. Hansberry died of cancer just six years later, at age thirty-four, but her stories, poems, essays, and dramatic works, which reflect her political passions and personal turmoil during the civil rights era, show no sign of fading away. Multiple biographers have considered what it meant to be "young, gifted, and Black" (in Hansberry's resonant phrase) at a time when mobs threatened her family for moving into a white Chicago neighborhood.[1] And innumerable productions of *A Raisin in the Sun* have established it as a key American document, comparable to Martin Luther King Jr.'s "I Have a Dream" speech.

Lorraine was seven when racists hurled rocks through her family's window for daring to live among whites. She drew on the memory for *A Raisin in the Sun,* in which Chicago's Younger family aspires to leave its rat-trap tenement building for a home of its own, thanks to a fateful life-insurance payout. The play transcends familiar types and tropes to seek the reality of Black lives. Rather than idealizing her characters, Hansberry goes straight for the pain points: the gender, religious, generational, and political divisions that threaten to tear their relationships apart.

It's an artistic approach she discovered during her two years at the University of Wisconsin. In 1948, Hansberry made the unconventional choice of attending a majority-white school in the snowy

Midwest rather than a historically Black college in the South. The decision brought a set of challenges. UW residence halls traditionally barred Black students, but Lorraine set her sights on a women's dormitory called Langdon Manor. She charmed the residents during an interview, received unanimous approval, and began forging close bonds with her new white roommates.

Hansberry also threw herself into political causes, developing a sophisticated critique of racial, sexual, and class oppression. She became a regular at local demonstrations with her handcrafted protest signs and served as president of the Young Progressives of America. A campus appearance by the nonconformist architect Frank Lloyd Wright, who sharply berated the university administrators sitting right in front of him, offered her an unforgettable lesson in speaking truth to power.

While engaging with everything and everyone around her, Hansberry also grappled with depression. Aimlessness set in during her freshman year. It was a trip to the theater—a campus production of Sean O'Casey's *Juno and the Paycock*—that suggested a new direction.

Hansberry watched the play's impoverished Irish characters speak to one another with a kind of workaday poetry. O'Casey didn't tidy up their lives but instead let them make their messes. They struggled and strived in a low-rent tenement, squabbling over a promised pile of money—a scenario Lorraine would later make her own in *A Raisin in the Sun*.

After this epiphany, Hansberry practically gave up on coursework and pivoted toward theater, acting in Aristophanes's *Lysistrata* and Federico García Lorca's *Yerma*. At the end of her sophomore year in 1950, she left the university for New York City to pursue what she called "an education of another kind": a cultural immersion in bohemian Greenwich Village that led to her career as a playwright.[2]

And yet the Wisconsin experience left an impression. In a diary entry written during her first year in New York City, she called Madison "a grey world I did terribly love through the awful hurt."[3]

24

Dickey Chapelle

The Trouble She Asked For

It all started with a fence in Shorewood. Young Dickey Chapelle (then known as Georgette Meyer) wanted to walk on top of it and look down on her mother's roses. The adults said no, but Dickey got up there anyway, risking her neck to see the world from a new vantage point.

Chapelle tells that story in her memoir, 1962's *What's a Woman Doing Here?*, originally titled *The Trouble I've Asked For*. The photojournalist spent her career in places women weren't supposed to be, dodging bullets to report from World War II, the 1956 Hungarian uprising, the Cuban revolution, and the Vietnam War, among other conflicts. Her role model was polar explorer Richard Byrd, the subject of a documentary fifteen-year-old Georgette snuck off to see at Milwaukee's Oriental Theatre. Byrd's fearlessness touched her so deeply that she later called herself "Dickey" in his honor.

Growing up in the Milwaukee area, Chapelle found that the quickest route to adventure was the Curtiss-Wright airport, where she spent time in the 1930s after dropping out of the Massachusetts Institute of Technology. She loved watching the stunt pilots at Sunday afternoon air shows and wrangled her way into working as the airport secretary in exchange for flying lessons. She also wrote articles about aviation for local newspapers. Nearsightedness stymied her career as a pilot, but her curiosity and courage made her a natural-born journalist.

Chapelle worked as a World War II correspondent after the attack on Pearl Harbor, developing her skills as a writer and photographer. She survived sniper fire at the battle of Iwo Jima and

Dickey Chapelle, pictured in Milwaukee in 1959 (her favorite photograph of herself at work), made it her mission to enter war zones considered too dangerous for women. WHI IMAGE ID 1942

took a gruesomely intimate photo—among her most famous—of a wounded marine lying on his back with a glazed expression. As she had done with her fence-walking capers in Shorewood, she disobeyed orders to get to where she wanted to be. When she defied a ban on female correspondents at the battle of Okinawa, a general shouted, "Get the broad the hell out of here!"[1]

Chapelle took these risks not as a daredevil but as an idealist. She'd adopted her family's pacifist convictions and believed in exposing the truth about what she called "the wreckage resulting from man's inhumanity to man." She wanted to tell stories of "men brave enough to risk their lives in the defense of freedom against tyranny."[2]

In the 1950s and '60s, Chapelle worked the front lines in her signature pearl earrings, Australian bush hat, and harlequin glasses. While covering the Hungarian revolution, she fell into Soviet hands and spent two months in prison. She won a 1963 award from the National Press Photographers Association for a shot of a marine suited up for combat in Vietnam, exposing the Pentagon's lie that US military personnel were serving only as advisers.

On November 4, 1965, Chapelle was covering a Marine search-and-destroy mission in Vietnam when the unit walked into a booby-trap and shrapnel hit her in the neck. A fellow photographer captured an image of her curled up in the brush, covered in blood, with her trademark bush hat lying where it had fallen. In the heart-wrenching photograph, she receives last rites from a chaplain as three marines look on, with God knows what going through their minds. As she lay dying, Chapelle reportedly said, "I guess it was bound to happen."[3]

Perhaps this was, in the words of her memoir's original title, the trouble she'd asked for. But, given her determination to uncover the truth in places where it needed to be found, we should all be grateful that she did.

25

Eudora Welty

The Icy World

Eudora Welty wrote short stories and novels set in her native Mississippi, evoking the humid Delta region so vividly you can almost hear the mosquitoes buzzing in your ears. Welty rooted herself in this landscape and spent most of her life in the Jackson house where she'd grown up. "I chose to live at home to do my writing in a familiar world and have never regretted it," she said, looking back on a literary career that earned her a Pulitzer Prize, National Book Critics Circle Award, American Book Award, multiple O. Henry Awards, and the Presidential Medal of Freedom.[1] In "Why I Live at the P.O.," "A Worn Path," "Petrified Man," and other enduring tales, she details the attitudes and aches of a very particular place.

So it may come as a surprise to learn that, from 1927 to 1929, this quintessential Southern writer had a crucial experience in Wisconsin.

After starting at the Mississippi State College for Women, eighteen-year-old Welty desired a change of scene. She hoped to stay in the South, but when Virginia's Randolph-Macon Woman's College turned her down, she went with her second choice: Madison's University of Wisconsin, in what she later called "the icy world."

It proved a revelatory two years. Welty's first shock came in a drawing class, where a model "lightly dropped her robe and stood, before us and a little above us, holding herself perfectly contained, in her full self and naked," she wrote in her memoir, *One Writer's Beginnings*, noting the contrast with her conservative art classes in Mississippi.[2]

Welty made friends, drank bathtub gin that tasted like dandruff shampoo, and acquired the nickname "Hunky." Still, she felt timid around the northerners who seemed to her like "sticks of flint." She languished in her math and education courses and mostly kept her distance from the campus literary scene, even while trying her hand at fiction and poetry. When she turned in a novel as a thesis require-ment, the future grande dame of American letters received a mere B.

"I could feel such a heavy heart inside me," she wrote in *One Writer's Beginnings*. "It was more than the pangs of growing up. . . . It was some kind of desire to be shown that the human spirit was not like that shivery winter in Wisconsin, that the opposite to all this existed in full."

The opposite did exist, and Welty stumbled across it at the UW library. Wandering in the stacks, she paged through a book that lay open on a table by the Irish writer George William Russell. It was, she said, like "being enveloped in a sea." In the same stacks, she found a volume of poems by William Butler Yeats and read all of them at once, standing by a window as the snow fell. She felt she could plunge into this poetry the way she might plunge into the snow—that she could "move in it, live in it."

In one of her English classes, gifted professor Ricardo Quintana helped Welty understand what made writers like Yeats and Russell special. In a word, *passion*.

She carried this lesson back to Mississippi along with her English degree. The professor who gave her thesis a B may have failed to recognize a prodigy, but Welty's fellow students proved more perceptive. As one Madison friend predicted, "You will be famous with your novel some day."[3]

Ya think?

26

Orson Welles

Hysteria Sweeps Country!

Orson Welles was born in Kenosha and had pivotal experiences in Madison. Though he didn't live in Wisconsin for long, the one-of-a-kind radio, film, and theatrical star called himself "a confirmed Badger."[1]

Welles directed, wrote, and acted in highly personal, visually dazzling, formally inventive movies such as *The Magnificent Ambersons* and *A Touch of Evil*. In his tour de force, 1941's *Citizen Kane*, he plays troubled newspaper tycoon Charles Foster Kane, who mysteriously mutters "Rosebud" on his deathbed. At the end, we learn that the word conjures a traumatic childhood memory and represents the key to Kane's soul.

Anyone looking for a Rosebud moment in Welles's own life might focus on the rainy, miserable day he attended his mother's funeral in Kenosha at age nine. A year later, after he moved to Madison, a *Capital Times* reporter heard rumors of a prodigy at Washington Elementary School and went to interview him. The article cited Welles's precocious reading habits, cartooning prowess, and storytelling gifts, calling him "an apparent genius." The paper printed an excerpt from Welles's poem "The Passing of a Lord" and cited his vocabulary, which included "a surprising number of large words equal to those of the average adult."[2]

The boy showed other signs of greatness during his yearlong stay in Madison. In the summer before fourth grade, he stood out at Madison's Camp Indianola, on the shore of Lake Mendota. Other campers scratched their heads when he showed up with his own easel and oil paints. He told such long-winded stories at campfires that counselor Lowell Frautschi struggled to shut him up.

But the budding artist would not be silenced. At the end of the summer session, Welles begged to put on a one-boy show of *Dr. Jekyll and Mr. Hyde*. With just a pair of glasses, a pitcher, two chairs, and a table as props, he convincingly transformed from one character to another using body language and vocal inflections. Those who witnessed the spectacle never forgot it. Decades later, Frautschi still spoke of the performance with awe, calling it "truly amazing."[3]

The rest of the country soon discovered Welles's genius when, in his early twenties, he conquered the New York City theater scene with visionary productions of *Caesar* and *Macbeth*. And then came his *War of the Worlds* broadcast, which caused a national panic on October 30, 1938.

With his Mercury Theatre troupe, actor-director Welles staged the story of a Martian invasion as a real-time account. His masterstroke was fabricating news bulletins that interrupted what sounded like regularly scheduled programming. Things turned grim during a bulletin from Grover's Mill, New Jersey, when "a reporter" offered a chilling account of a Martian emerging from its spaceship.

Welles was directing the cast and orchestra from a podium in CBS's Manhattan studio. As the monster made its appearance, he signaled for complete silence, which lasted for six bloodcurdling seconds. Listeners got the idea that everyone in Grover's Mill, plus all the recording equipment, had evaporated in a Martian heat ray.

Outside the studio, all hell broke loose. Some Americans packed up their belongings and fled their homes. Others sought refuge in police stations and pressed clothing to their mouths to protect against the Martians' poison smoke. The next day, the *Wisconsin State Journal*'s front-page headline typified newspaper coverage around the world: "Hysteria Sweeps Country as Radio Hoax Describes Invasion by Mars Giants!" The government launched an investigation, and Congress threatened to censor radio.

In the CBS studio, Orson Welles wreaked havoc with his 1938 *War of the Worlds* radio broadcast, mischievously simulating a Martian invasion.
DALLAS DISPATCH-JOURNAL, OCTOBER 31, 1938

Many had missed the second half of the broadcast as they abandoned their radios in terror. But those who stuck it out heard a final word from the twenty-three-year-old prankster. While panicked callers overwhelmed the CBS switchboard, Welles informed anyone still listening that his little radio play had been all in good fun: "This is Orson Welles, ladies and gentlemen, out of character to assure you that *The War of The Worlds* has no further significance than as the holiday offering it was intended to be—the Mercury Theatre's own radio version of dressing up in a sheet and jumping out of a bush and saying boo."[4]

Wherever they happened to be, Welles's former bunkmates at Camp Indianola were surely smiling.

27

Kevin Henkes and Laura Dronzek

A Storybook Romance

Before computers, children's book illustrators typically drew or painted on paper, then delivered their pages to publishers by mail or in person. Today, it's more common for artists to create images onscreen and submit the final product electronically. While software has its advantages, something essential may be lost in the transition to gigabytes. Brushstrokes, smudges, drips—a human touch.

In a cozy Madison home, husband-and-wife artists Kevin Henkes and Laura Dronzek preserve the old ways. They work in separate attic studios, sometimes comparing notes on individual projects and sometimes collaborating. Henkes's studio has no computer, but instead boasts a manual typewriter and art supplies still in use from his Racine childhood, including a sturdy Mickey Mouse light-up desk. Dronzek's studio overflows with finished canvases and works in progress, both for children's books and exhibitions. Whenever I visit them there, I have the thrill of peeking at new classics constantly under construction.

After Henkes and Dronzek complete a project, they pack up the handcrafted pages and send them to a publisher in New York City. A human being delivers them to an editor's desk—a gift to unwrap, hold in the hand, and marvel over, rather than simply an attachment to click on.

In the 1960s, Henkes grew up in the children's section of the Racine library, entranced by Ruth Krauss and Crockett Johnson's *The Carrot Seed*, Julian Scheer and Marvin Bileck's *Rain Makes Applesauce*, and other inventive children's books. He excelled in both writing and drawing and began winning prizes at local art fairs. A perceptive teacher told him, "I wouldn't be surprised to see a book with your name on it one day."[1] It was a formative moment: permission to dream of a previously unimaginable future.

At the University of Wisconsin–Madison, Henkes found mentors in the art department and the Cooperative Children's Book Center. With his eye on the prize, he immersed himself in drawing, typography, and children's literature, working on a book called *All Alone* in one of his UW classes. In the summer of 1980, the determined nineteen-year-old made appointments with top children's publishers in New York City. Greenwillow Books editor Susan Hirschman took one look at his portfolio and knew she'd struck gold.

Henkes's publishing career began quietly with *All Alone*, in which a solitary child discovers the power of his imagination— clearly a subject close to home. But his books didn't stay quiet for long. Indeed, some of them veritably squeaked. *Chrysanthemum*, *Lilly's Purple Plastic Purse*, *Owen*, and *Wemberly Worried* ushered readers into a universe of endearing mice who—despite curling tails and big pink ears—experienced the same problems as their human counterparts. With witty images and sly storytelling, they reflected children's hopes and fears. Henkes also wrote *Sweeping Up the Heart*, *Olive's Ocean*, *The Year of Billy Miller*, and other novels for young readers, notable for their rich figurative language and exquisite shades of feeling.

Dronzek grew up about an hour from Henkes in Deerfield, Illinois, with a similar love of children's books. She had an artist's eye, studying Garth Williams's serene animal imagery in *Charlotte's Web* and Maurice Sendak's in *Mr. Rabbit and the Lovely Present*. She put off enrolling in an art class until her last undergraduate semester at UW–Madison, instead majoring in English and psychology. But the paintbrush beckoned. She kept taking art classes, earned an MFA in painting at the UW, and soon began placing her work in galleries and museums. While finding herself, she also found the love of her life.

Henkes and Dronzek met in Madison, married, and had two children. Their artistic collaboration began in 1999, when Dronzek provided lush winter images for Henkes's rhythmic text in *Oh!* She turned landscapes into dreamscapes, with a painterly palette and a vision of children and animals in peaceful coexistence. Dronzek illustrated books by other authors, including George Shannon's *White Is for Blueberry* and Helen V. Griffith's *Moonlight*. But her collaborations with Henkes—as in *Birds, Summer Song,* and *Winter Is Here*—produce a special kind of magic.

In each project, the artists see the world with new eyes. Decades after his breakthrough mouse books, Henkes continues to write and illustrate masterpieces (including *Kitten's First Full Moon* and *Waiting*) that find him penetrating deeper into childhood consciousness even as he moves farther from it chronologically. He's also picked up a Caldecott Medal, two Newbery Honors, and the Children's Literature Legacy Award, the industry's highest accolade for a body of work.

Meanwhile, Dronzek grows ever more skillful at bringing a fine-art sensibility to children's books. The opening spread of *Winter Is Here* arranges seventeen people and six animals in harmonious balance, with planes artfully delineated by a lake, jutting branches, and a diagonal road that thrusts across the two pages. A line of three children pulling sleds up a hill creates a rhythmic effect, echoed by three houses in the distance. Red caps, coats, scarves, and boots stand out against the white snow, which shimmers with a heavy undercoat of blue and purple. The visible brushstrokes add texture and conjure an image of the pigment-stained artist at her easel. You feel like running your finger across the page to see if you can actually touch the bumps and ridges.

The painting is paradoxical: complex yet simple. Such are the mysteries of the human touch.

28

Georgia O'Keeffe

Sun Prairie's Defiant Daughter

Raised on a Sun Prairie farm, Georgia O'Keeffe emerged as a boldly original painter in the early twentieth century with her idiosyncratic vision of desert landscapes and flowers. The curves and folds of her abstract lilies seduced viewers into feeling an intimate connection with nature.

By the 1970s, the world knew O'Keeffe as an artist who pursued her own vision and a woman who lived on her own terms. Unfortunately, Sun Prairie misjudged her independent spirit when it decided to boost its image as her birthplace. After naming a park after her, the city asked O'Keeffe to appear in its 1976 bicentennial parade and donate a painting to its historical museum.

Unsurprisingly, Georgia turned them down on both counts. She was, after all, in her eighties, and getting to Sun Prairie from her isolated home in Abiquiu, New Mexico, would have proved difficult. She was also going blind and not keen on letting people know it. As for donating a priceless painting—well, that's an iffy request for any artist of her stature.

But Sun Prairie took the refusal as a snub and, in 1977, renamed the park. It's a shame that things turned sour, because O'Keeffe always appreciated her roots. She believed Wisconsin forged her strong will and prepared her to break through barriers in a male-dominated field.

Born in 1887, Georgia grew up in a family of women who stood shoulder to shoulder with men, making their way in a rugged rural outpost. With a determination typical of her clan, she set her sights on an artistic career at age ten and wowed her teachers at Madison's

Sacred Heart Academy with drawings and watercolors. By the time she moved to the East Coast with her family at age fifteen, she had developed the unconventional personality that would grab the world's attention. This iconoclast never dressed, behaved, or painted according to any fashion.

When O'Keeffe settled in a wild part of New Mexico in 1949, she contended with rattlesnakes and flash floods. The region had no telephones, no grocery stores, and no medical services. Her New York City friends wondered how she survived in such harsh conditions, but in response, O'Keeffe pointed to her origins in Wisconsin—a place, she said, where people worked with their hands.

O'Keeffe's hometown changed its tune after she died in 1986, honoring her with a historical marker, exhibitions, and special events. The independent spirit that hurt feelings in 1976 is now a source of civic pride—and why not, since she acquired it right there in Sun Prairie?

29

Beth Nguyen

Beefaroni Meets Bánh Chưng

Beth Nguyen arrived in the United States as an infant in 1975 when her father fled the communists who overran Saigon at the end of the Vietnam War. As the child of a refugee, she spent her youth in Grand Rapids, Michigan, with one foot in the old world and the other in a Burger King. And that was the start of an identity crisis. At home, Beth (or Bich, as she was called) celebrated Tết and sucked on chilled lychees. At school and at friends' houses, she ate Chef Boyardee spaghetti and learned the words to Olivia Newton-John's "Physical." Was she Vietnamese? American? Both? Neither?

We know that Nguyen survived her traumas, becoming an American Book Award–winning novelist for *Short Girls* and joining the University of Wisconsin–Madison's creative writing faculty. And yet we feel her anguish in *Stealing Buddha's Dinner*, a 2007 memoir of her conflicted childhood. Will she overcome what she describes as the "embarrassment and shame that always lay in wait"? The "intense shyness that wore me out daily"? Will she find a way into what she calls "the club of girlhood" despite feeling alienated from everyone and everything around her?[1]

Grand Rapids proclaims itself "An All-American City," and young Bich can't tell if that's a promise, a threat, or a warning. She is a short, dark-haired girl in a population of tall blonds, with a home life unlike any she's seen on American television. The family never discusses her birth mother, who was left behind in Vietnam during the chaotic escape. Her grandmother leaves plates of fruit for their dead ancestors beneath a golden Buddha statue that sits on a high shelf. Her father speaks imperfect English and struggles to provide for the extended family with his grimy factory job at the North American Feather Company. The household's cultural dynamics grow even more confusing when he marries a strong-willed woman, who adds her own Mexican cuisine to the daily fare of canh chua, bánh chưng, and chả giò.

Bich obsesses over food, partly because she doesn't get enough of it. But more than that, the products she sees on TV commercials and in schoolmates' lunchboxes promise entrée into mainstream American life. She covets what seemingly normal Americans eat so she can be normal, too. The loving descriptions of junk food in *Stealing Buddha's Dinner* establish Nguyen as the bard of Beefaroni and Bubble Yum. "The Pringles glowed by window light, their fine curvatures nearly translucent," she observes, attuned to every taste and texture. "So delicate, breaking into salty shards on our tongues." A disapproving elder accuses Bich's eyes of being bigger than her stomach—and, indeed, it's hard to imagine a stomach big enough for this girl's spiritual hunger.

The memoir is at once specific—Vietnam-meets-the-Midwest in the Madonna-era 1980s—and universal. As the grandson of Eastern European Jewish immigrants, I can relate to Nguyen's tales of eating ethnic food and practicing arcane customs behind closed doors. I, too, noticed how comfortably everyone but me appeared to fit into sports, clubs, and holiday pageants. And so I cheered Bich's halting progress from self-consciousness to self-assertion. The instrument of her transformation is literature; *Harriet the Spy, Little House in the Big Woods*, and other narratives about observant outsiders help her piece together a personality. She comes into her own as the bookish kid at peace with being different. "I could read myself out of Grand Rapids," she realizes, foreshadowing her life at UW–Madison as a renowned author and professor.

When she reached Wisconsin in her adulthood, Nguyen had a new perspective on her journey, which she chronicled in the 2023 memoir *Owner of a Lonely Heart*. She portrays herself at her desk in Madison, gazing out the window at dusk and "writing in and into the darkness."[2] As a mother of two struggling to reconnect with her birth mom, Nguyen is still puzzling over her identity. At the same time, there's no doubt about what she has become: an artist.

30

Edna Ferber

"I Wouldn't Burn That If I Were You"

Edna Ferber's novels, stories, and plays connected with Americans as sexual politics evolved in the early twentieth century. The strong heroines of *So Big, Show Boat, Cimarron, Giant,* and *Stage Door* suited an era when women demanded voting rights and personal autonomy. Ferber drew on her experience as a Wisconsin journalist to create closely observed settings and characters that lent themselves to big-screen adaptations. Her fierce wit also made her a natural for the Algonquin Round Table, where she supped and sparred with New York City's literary giants at the famed Algonquin Hotel. Ferber won a Pulitzer Prize and a solid-gold epitaph from the *New York Times*: "greatest woman novelist of her day."[1] And yet, before her literary career even got off the ground, it almost went up in flames in an Appleton furnace.

Edna moved to Appleton in 1897 at age twelve when her family got fed up with antisemitic treatment in Ottumwa, Iowa. Right off the bat, she impressed the townsfolk with her overactive imagination. Young Edna envisioned a life on the stage and—faking an Italian accent—regaled schoolmates with tales of her made-up boyfriend, Joe. She barreled through Ryan High School, writing for the newspaper, acting in plays, and winning the state declamatory contest. However, her dream of studying theater at Chicago's Northwestern University foundered along with her family's finances. The Ferbers ran a general store and struggled to make ends meet when her father's health declined. Instead of going to college, Edna had to pitch in by taking a job—and luckily, an editor at the *Appleton Daily Crescent* happened to see her sparkling senior essay.

In 1903, seventeen-year-old Ferber became the first female reporter in the *Daily Crescent* newsroom. For three dollars a week, she covered local goings-on with stylistic flourishes that stood out in an otherwise prosaic publication. When hometown hero Harry Houdini toured through Appleton, she cornered the athletic escape artist at a College Avenue drugstore. In the ensuing article, she charmingly informed readers what his forearm felt like: "as massive and hard as a granite pillar."[2]

Ferber's bosses raised her weekly salary to five dollars, then eight dollars, and published this testimonial: "One of the brightest young women of this city, Miss Edna Jessica Ferber, gives promise of becoming one of the best newspaperwomen in the state."[3] Nevertheless, the *Daily Crescent* ended its experiment with a coed newsroom after two years, exasperated by Ferber's tendency toward embellishment. Undaunted, she took a job at the *Milwaukee Journal* for fifteen dollars a week and reveled in big-city life.

But in 1909, the revelry caught up with her. Overworked and feeling guilty about abandoning her invalid father, Ferber suffered a nervous collapse and returned home to Appleton to recuperate. The respite gave her the chance to find her true calling. Buying a secondhand typewriter, she used two fingers to tap out her first short story, a playful satire of romance fiction called "The Homely Heroine." She mailed it off to the national publication *Everybody's Magazine* and promptly received an acceptance. That encouraged her to try her hand at a novel, and she penned *Dawn O'Hara, the Girl Who Laughed* based on her experiences as a Milwaukee journalist. She found no takers and, discouraged, set the manuscript aside.

In the meantime, Ferber's father died, and her family packed up to leave Appleton for new horizons in Chicago. They began making trips to the furnace to burn the things they didn't need. Edna prepared to feed *Dawn O'Hara, the Girl Who Laughed* into the flames when her mother took the pages out of her hands.

"I wouldn't burn that if I were you," she said. "Keep it."

"Nobody wants it," Edna replied.

After her stint as a pioneering Wisconsin journalist, Edna Ferber, pictured around 1939, recreated herself as a novelist—one of the greatest of her time. WISCONSIN CENTER FOR FILM AND THEATER RESEARCH

"You never can tell," Mom insisted, setting the soon-to-be-popular novel in the don't-burn pile. "Maybe you haven't sent it to the right person."[4]

And so Edna Ferber departed Appleton, manuscript in her suitcase. Like one of her intrepid heroines, she was ready to meet her destiny.

31

Joyce Carol Oates

The Upside of Failure

Joyce Carol Oates has made a career of examining American life—pretty much all of it. In hundreds of realist novels, gothic novels, young adult novels, poems, short stories, plays, and essays, she shows how people from sea to shining sea "forge their own souls," for good or ill.[1] Her fiction imagines characters with complex inner lives, often placing them in violent settings: the desperate Detroit of *them* or the seamier-than-it-seems small town of *We Were the Mulvaneys*. It also reimagines historical figures doomed by sinister social forces, such as Chappaquiddick victim Mary Jo Kopechne in *Black Water* or Marilyn Monroe in *Blonde*. Indeed, Oates's imagination is an engine that never quits, and it lifted her from an impoverished childhood in Millersport, New York, to literary fame.

Yet she may never have reached such heights if she hadn't failed spectacularly as a Madison graduate student.

The gift of a typewriter launched fourteen-year-old Joyce's career as a writer, and one can envision steam pouring off the keys as she typed, even in junior high. She kept up the pace at Syracuse University and won a *Mademoiselle* story contest as an undergraduate. But as the first member of her family even to finish high school, she couldn't conceive of fiction writing as a career. Instead, she headed to the University of Wisconsin in 1960 to earn a PhD in English so she could teach at the college level. In grad school, she speculated, she would pursue her other love—reading—and dabble in fiction on the side.

Alas, the UW English department did not approach literature with love. The hidebound faculty viewed texts not as awe-inspiring masterpieces, but as historical documents in need of footnotes. Lots and lots of footnotes. Oates felt her soul shriveling as she labored under a patriarchal system that discouraged her fanciful ideas in favor of academic drudgery. When she daringly compared sixteenth-century poet Edmund Spenser and twentieth-century experimentalist Franz Kafka, her tut-tutting professor demanded that she take a more traditional approach with, you guessed it, more footnotes. "The thrilling emotional punch of great art—totally beyond the range of these earnest scholarly individuals," she later wrote in her essay "Nighthawk: Recollections of a Lost Time."[2]

Worst of all, dabbling in fiction proved to be a pipe dream. There wasn't time—not while studying arcane religious controversies in Renaissance England. At twenty-two, she had never seriously examined her urge to tell stories, but now that she couldn't tell them, panic set in. It was the equivalent, she felt, of "ceasing to dream, or to breathe."[3]

Oates suffered bouts of insomnia. While others slept, she wandered from her tiny room in Barnard Hall to choppy Lake Mendota, where she fought off thoughts of going under. Not even meeting and quickly marrying fellow UW grad student Raymond Smith could cure what she called "the malaise of Madison."[4]

At the end of the academic year, Oates faced a tribunal of dour male faculty members for her master's exam. She prepared to discourse knowledgeably about her beloved Emily Dickinson and Walt Whitman but instead faced pedantic questions about dates and drafts. With no answers forthcoming, the harsh verdict arrived: yes to a master's degree but no to continuing for the PhD. Joyce Carol Oates herself would become a footnote in the history of the University of Wisconsin.

Only later did she come to understand the triumph hidden in this failure. As an academic, she might never have written the books she was born to write. The university came to understand this, too, semi-apologizing by granting her an honorary doctorate long after she'd won a National Book Award. Oates returned to campus to accept the degree in 1985, finally at peace. "In Madison," she thought, "I have been made to feel at last that I do belong."[5]

And she felt something even more profound: the sense that people can transcend defeat. That they can redefine themselves. That they can reemerge.

32

Frank Lloyd Wright and Pedro Guerrero

Buildings as Sculpture

Richland Center–born Frank Lloyd Wright pioneered organic architecture, bringing his buildings into harmony with people and places. His innovative use of materials and space in Fallingwater, the Guggenheim Museum, and other startling structures marked him as one of the twentieth century's great iconoclasts, following his muse with little concern for critics or creditors.

Pedro Guerrero became Wright's chosen photographer, producing the best-known images of both the architect and his art. They met in 1939 when, as a twenty-two-year-old college dropout in Mesa, Arizona, Guerrero got up the nerve to apply for a job with Wright in nearby Scottsdale. Hard at work building his winter headquarters, Taliesin West, Wright saw promise in Guerrero's portfolio of nudes and still lifes. The architect hired the stunned young man on the spot and instructed him to chronicle the dramatic structures taking shape in the Arizona desert.

Guerrero marveled over the unconventional forms, which matched those of the surrounding mountains. The colors and textures mirrored the rocky ground. Using an unwieldly five-by-seven camera, with no shutter and just one lens, he judged the position of the sun and strove to show the patterns, shadows, and angles to best effect.

After a few months of learning on the job, Guerrero packed up his bedroll to accompany Wright back to his home base, the Spring Green compound called Taliesin. On the drive, the young man drank in the southwestern Wisconsin panorama that had inspired Wright's Prairie Style architecture, with its gentle hills, flat valleys,

Iconoclastic architect Frank Lloyd Wright (left) with his like-
minded photographer, Pedro Guerrero, in 1949. © THE ESTATE
OF PEDRO E. GUERRERO

and neat farmhouses. Then came Guerrero's first sight of Taliesin,
a sandstone and cypress wonderland nestled into the landscape
near the Wisconsin River. It was a visual artist's dream, and he set
about photographing the estate's buildings as if they were sculpture. His vision closely matched Wright's, so to look at these images
is to know exactly how the architect wanted his work to be seen.

Wright so respected Guerrero's craftsmanship—and Guerrero himself—that he took him along to document other projects around Wisconsin. On these jaunts, the observant photographer collected amusing stories he would tell for the rest of his life. Among other eccentricities, Wright discouraged clients from expressing their own tastes once they occupied his houses. He shamelessly rearranged their furniture and instructed Guerrero to destroy any knickknacks that detracted from Wright's pure artistic conception.

Guerrero left Spring Green to serve in World War II and then to shoot for glossy magazines and major artists on the East Coast. But he remained Wright's preferred photographer, making himself available for on-call projects until the architect's death in 1959. After that, Guerrero frequently returned to Wisconsin, spending summers in Mineral Point and treating local admirers to tales of his larger-than-life mentor. As one of those admirers, I can report that, on the serious subject of Frank Lloyd Wright, no one on earth was funnier.

When Guerrero died in 2012 at age ninety-five, he was buried in the little cemetery across the road from Taliesin. Wright was buried there, too, until his widow ordered his remains shipped to Taliesin West in 1985. The original marker still stands, however, and it's fitting that Wright's gravestone and Guerrero's will spend eternity in Wisconsin, side by side.

33

Jane Hamilton

The Author and the Apples

On Saturday mornings, patrons of the Dane County Farmers' Market on Madison's Capitol Square line up for apples at the Ela Orchard booth. I sometimes work there myself, selling sweet Macouns, tart Cortlands, and other lovingly tended heirloom varieties, plus an unpasteurized cider so delectable that supplies run out well before noon closing time. Many people come simply to converse with Ela's Jane Hamilton as she hands out bags heavy with the week's harvest and flashes a smile some might recognize from her *Oprah Winfrey Show* appearances. Rarely is a famous author so accessible to her adoring public.

Hamilton's journey to the Rochester-based orchard is the stuff of Wisconsin legend. She immersed herself in dance in her hometown of Oak Park, Illinois, but turned to thoughts of a writing career in the 1970s at Minnesota's Carleton College. After graduation, she headed toward New York City with two hundred dollars in her pocket to start an internship at Dell Publishing. On the way, however, she stopped at the orchard with a college classmate whose family ran the place. Sparks flew between her and Ela's Bob Willard, and Dell promptly lost its intern. Jane and Bob married, and she pursued that writing career from the unlikely location of a farmhouse in Racine County.

Well, unlikely for anyone but Hamilton, whose work ethic matched that of fellow Oak Park native Ernest Hemingway. She had an eye for detail, an ear for conversation, and a talent for seeing into the heart of people and places. It didn't take long for *Harper's Magazine* to accept one of her stories or for Ticknor and Fields to publish her first novel, *The Book of Ruth* (1988), about a beleaguered woman and her brutal family. The book won the PEN/Hemingway Award for Debut Novel and became a selection for Oprah's Book Club. A literary star—one who picked apples on the side—was born.

Hamilton rendered uncannily vivid Wisconsin settings, characters, and conflicts in subsequent novels: *Laura Rider's Masterpiece*, *Disobedience*, and *A Map of the World* (also selected for Winfrey's book club and adapted as a movie starring Sigourney Weaver). But the book closest to home—literally her own backyard—was 2016's *The Excellent Lombards*.

Narrator Mary Frances Lombard recounts her childhood in an apple orchard paradise that would be familiar to Adam and Eve. At least, that's how it looks to Mary Frances during prepubescence, when her father bends nature to his will and her brother serves as a gallant protector. But we all know what happened to Adam and Eve, and Mary Frances, too, travels the thorny path from innocence to experience, perceiving the flaws in her fairy-tale family. Still, she clings to her youthful vision of inheriting the farm and preserving it as a peaceable kingdom, even as an orderly succession seems increasingly unlikely.

The Excellent Lombards finds Hamilton at the height of her powers. The book's effortless rhythm and grace recall her background as a dancer. The sentences take surprising turns, like a winding country road, and often arrive at punchlines that leave you laughing out loud. The novel satirizes parents, teachers, cheerleaders, town boards, and even sheep too trusting to realize they're being led to slaughter. Hamilton keeps the playfulness and poignancy in perfect balance, delivering an emotional wallop free from sentimentality.

Ela Orchard apples are delicious, but after *The Excellent Lombards*, they'll be forever freighted with myth, much like the one from the Garden of Eden.

34

Helen Farnsworth Mears

Genius of Wisconsin

Imagine a child growing up in 1870s Oshkosh obsessed with forms. As a toddler, Helen Farnsworth Mears bit pieces of bread into the shapes of horses and dogs. She mucked about with mud, dough, putty, and tar, molding lumps into likenesses. When she finally got hold of a more traditional artistic medium—clay—she created startlingly accurate images of her neighbors.

Helen's parents could see that she was not like the other children on Parkway Avenue. Her father had studied surgery, so he taught her what he knew about anatomy. He also converted a backyard shed into a studio and made Helen special sculpting tools. At age nine, she crafted a head of Apollo, baked it in the family oven, and won a prize at the Winnebago County Fair.

Mears took a few steps toward a conventional career by attending the Oshkosh State Normal School for teacher training. But she couldn't keep her hands out of the clay. After a brief stint at the Art Institute of Chicago, she received a major commission: a sculpture to represent Wisconsin at the 1893 Chicago World's Fair. The young artist delivered the nine-foot-tall *Genius of Wisconsin*, in which a female figure perches on a craggy rock, one hand clutching her robe, the other resting on the head of an eagle that spreads its magnificent wings by her shoulder. Though the figure stands at ease, the sculpture exudes dynamism, with the robe's naturalistic folds straining against her bent knee. The eagle's rippling feathers suggest movement, and its outspread wings give the piece a horizontal thrust. Human, land, and animal exist in harmony, and the figure's upward gaze recalls the state's motto, "Forward." Indeed, this eagle seems ready to soar straight into the future.

The Milwaukee Woman's Club gave Mears a five-hundred-dollar prize for *Genius of Wisconsin*, enabling a trip to New York City to study at the Art Students League. Within two weeks, her work caught the attention of the prominent sculptor Augustus Saint-Gaudens, who hired her as an assistant. Next came two years of study in France and Italy, where she visited museums, exhibited in salons, and gained an international reputation.

Back in her New York studio, Mears took her place among the great American sculptors. Her three-panel bas-relief *The Fountain of Life* won a medal at the 1904 St. Louis World's Fair, and the Metropolitan Museum of Art displayed her 1906 bas-relief portrait of composer Edward MacDowell. She also returned to Wisconsin to create sculptural portraits of her mother and the president of the Oshkosh State Normal School. Her marble sculpture of suffragist Frances Willard earned high praise as the first statue of a woman placed in the US Capitol.

Even as Mears's avid supporter, Saint-Gaudens described her style with a touch of sexism, indicating what female artists were up against in the early twentieth century: "It has a man's strength, but the spiritual grace which only a woman's hand could lend it."[1]

Mears had come a long way from shaping bread with her teeth, but her fortunes took a turn in 1910, when she was commissioned for a sculpture to sit atop Wisconsin's Capitol dome. She created a model of a female figure with arms raised, but the commissioners didn't like it. She came up with another figure carrying a shield and a scepter. Again, the group said no. She tried one more time, but the commission never considered her third model, dropping Mears in favor of Daniel Chester French. He received $20,000 for his sculpture, while Mears got a nominal $1,500 for what she had considered a guaranteed contract.

This embarrassment—in her home state, no less—marked the beginning of the end. Mears struggled financially, despite working

Originally created for the 1893 Chicago World's
Fair, Helen Farnsworth Mears's sculpture *Genius
of Wisconsin* took its rightful place in the Wisconsin
Capitol after her tragic death. WHI IMAGE ID 82743

herself into exhaustion, and died destitute at age forty-three, with
unfinished works littering her studio. No one could afford a marker
for her grave in Oshkosh's Riverside Cemetery.

The *Madison Democrat* reported her death on February 19, 1916,
offering a bittersweet epitaph: "Her art, touched with the qualities
that had distinguished it from the first, a graciousness so deep it
could be mistaken for sadness, remained, after all her study, still in
spirit, the art of the Wisconsin child."[2]

Despite its tragic ending, Mears's story is inspiring: artist
emerges from small-town Wisconsin, follows her muse, and suc-
ceeds in a male-dominated field. It also has a fitting coda. Thanks
to a group of Wisconsin women, *Genius of Wisconsin* now resides in
the Wisconsin Capitol, right where it belongs.

35

Lorine Niedecker

Sworn to Water

Lorine Niedecker is Wisconsin's Emily Dickinson. Each woman forged her avant-garde poetry while living a solitary existence in an out-of-the-way place. Each drew inspiration from the natural world buzzing and blooming just outside her window. And each suffered neglect from her contemporaries, receiving widespread acclaim only after her death. But affluent Emily never had to scrub hospital floors for a living.

Niedecker grew up getting her shoes wet on Blackhawk Island, a waterlogged peninsula near Fort Atkinson where the Rock River feeds into Lake Koshkonong. The area's sounds, sights, and scents entranced her for a lifetime. "Nature is lush here," she wrote to an acquaintance. "I feel as tho I spent my childhood outdoors—redwinged blackbirds, willows, maples, boats, fishing (the smell of tarred nets), tittering and squawking noises from the marsh."[1]

Complementing the birdsong of her youth were the musical cadences of nursery rhymes recited by her grandfather. Teenage Lorine adored poetry, thanks to a Fort Atkinson High School teacher who introduced her to fellow nature lover William Wordsworth and the British Romantics. She read widely and graduated at the top of her class, heading south on Highway 26 to attend Beloit College in 1922. But her formal studies ended after two years when her father's business ventures fell apart due to his drinking.

Niedecker returned home, cared for her sickly mother, and took a menial job as a library assistant in Fort Atkinson. She also entered an abortive marriage to a Blackhawk Island farmer's son. Influenced by the direct, colloquial style of modernist poets Ezra Pound and

Avant-garde poet Lorine Niedecker, pictured in 1969, spent her life searching for universal truth in the marshes and mud of isolated Blackhawk Island. UNIVERSITY OF WISCONSIN–MADISON ARCHIVES, GAIL ROUB COLLECTION, 003.19.182

H.D., she published a couple of Imagist poems in small magazines, but after giving up her educational ambitions, she faced a bleak future.

Then fate came calling in the form of *Poetry* magazine—in particular, a 1931 issue devoted to a modernist style called Objectivism. Niedecker felt an instant affinity with the oblique, highly compressed stanzas of Louis Zukofsky and other urban intellectuals who based their poetry in precise observation. She commenced a correspondence with Zukofsky, moved to New York City, and began an affair with him. It didn't last long, but their artistic connection sustained her when she returned to Blackhawk Island to write poetry amid personal hardships.

This was the period of scrubbing floors at Fort Atkinson Memorial Hospital. She also worked as a stenographer and proofreader. Niedecker lived in a rough cottage with no telephone or indoor plumbing, interacting with Blackhawk Island neighbors who knew nothing of her single-minded obsession with experimental verse. ("What would they say if they knew / I sit for two months on six lines / of poetry?" she wrote.[2]) And yet, even in her marshy outpost, she maintained ties to literary circles by corresponding with Zukofsky and other poets and ordering hard-to-find books from the Fort Atkinson library.

Her efforts yielded few publications. Aside from her 1946 collection *New Goose*, Niedecker placed just a handful of poems in small magazines in the 1940s and '50s. Still, she never lost a sense of herself as an artist. She drew inspiration from her surroundings—"marsh mud / algae, equisetum, willows / sweet green / noisy birds and frogs"—as well as overheard gossip.[3] An interest in the subconscious compelled her to sleep with a pencil under her pillow so she could record her dreams for future use. She saw her imagination as a "condensery," transmuting sensory impressions, local speech, family history, and everything she read into spare verses.

A second marriage in the 1960s brought financial stability, allowing Niedecker to retire from manual labor and focus on poetry. She published two more volumes, *My Friend Tree* and *North Central*, as well as two editions of collected poems, *T&G* and *My Life by Water*. A handful of critics and poets recognized her genius (one admirer found his way to Blackhawk Island to make a precious tape-recording of Niedecker reading her work), but the rest of the world caught up only after her death in 1970.

Wisconsin is now proud of a poet who consciously chose Blackhawk Island over New York City and mined its marshes for universal truth. A 1991 state historical marker outside her cottage brags that her poems "ranked among the twentieth century's finest." The marker quotes from "Paean to Place," situating Niedecker firmly in that very spot: "Fish / fowl / flood / Water lily mud / My life / in the leaves and on water / My mother and I / born / in swale and swamp and sworn / to water."

36

Michael Mann

A Cinematic Obsession

At the University of Wisconsin, Michael Mann obsessed over what to do with his life. He'd grown up in Chicago, toiling as a short-order cook, cab driver, and construction worker. That plus his English degree would qualify him to be . . . what, exactly?

Moviemaking hadn't entered his mind. For a hardworking grocer's son with little time for artistic pursuits, how could it? But the university was beginning to offer courses in film history and theory in the early 1960s, giving Mann a look at German expressionism. The stylish imagery rocked him back on his heels—and then Stanley Kubrick's *Dr. Strangelove* delivered a knockout punch. He saw how a film could connect with a mainstream audience while also communicating an auteur's singular point of view. Mann's existential quest had come to an end. As he walked down Bascom Hill after one of these screenings, he knew he would make movies. Personal and popular ones, like *Dr. Strangelove*.

How many UW film students have had the same thought on the same hill? What distinguished Mann was his obsessiveness. With characteristic intensity, he tore through film school in London and was soon hired as a writer for the 1970s cop show *Starsky and Hutch*. He scored his first big success with 1979's made-for-television prison movie *The Jericho Mile*, which introduced the world to a writer-director who would take no half-measures in pursuit of a plot. Mann shot the picture on location in Folsom Prison, developed relationships with the convicts, and even cast some of them in minor roles. *The Jericho Mile* won three Emmy Awards and set the

Michael Mann (left) directed Steven Waddington (center) and Daniel Day-Lewis (right) in 1992's *The Last of the Mohicans,* one of his classic films about imperfect characters striving for perfection. WISCONSIN CENTER FOR FILM AND THEATER RESEARCH

stage for Mann's later cinematic triumphs, which stayed true to his long-ago vision on Bascom Hill.

Like the directors featured in his UW film classes, he developed a style of his own—one that might be called Mann-ly, with aggressive editing and audio used to evoke male protagonists on the edge. You know you're in the Michael Mann universe when a car speeds down a dark city street, neon reflecting on the windshield, synthesizers and electric guitars pulsating in time with the driver's dangerously elevated heartbeat. In his frequent tales of cops versus criminals (*Miami Vice, Thief, Heat, Manhunter, Collateral, Blackhat*), the gun battles can rattle your dental fillings thanks to Mann's penchant for using raw sound captured on set.

The immediacy makes these scenes hard to shrug off as superfluous violence. They involve viewers directly in the characters' fateful conflicts with the powers-that-be. Muhammad Ali (Will Smith) puts up his dukes against the entire US government in *Ali,* and TV news producer Lowell Bergman (Al Pacino) confronts crooked tobacco corporations in *The Insider*. Mann's characters are imperfect people striving for perfection in their work, whether as a hit man (Tom Cruise in *Collateral*) or a hacker (Chris Hemsworth in *Blackhat*). They may yearn for a normal existence, but their obsessions consign them to life on the margins.

Like any artist who swings for the fences, Mann occasionally strikes out. One of his misses, the 2009 gangster epic *Public Enemies*, is a loving tribute to Wisconsin, with location filming in Madison, Beaver Dam, Columbus, Darlington, Oshkosh, Baraboo, Milwaukee, and Manitowish Waters. But the script's grand psychological conceit—equating John Dillinger (Johnny Depp) with the lawman trying to stop him (Christian Bale)—is as shaky as Mann's handheld camera.

By contrast, the best Mann films, such as *Heat, Collateral, Ali, The Insider,* and *Thief,* perfectly combine mood, music, and moral concerns, rivaling masterpieces by his crime-focused peers Martin Scorsese and Francis Ford Coppola. They're sure to inspire future generations of moviemakers and fans, just as that Madison screening of *Dr. Strangelove* inspired young Michael Mann.

37

Zona Gale

The Home Folks and Neighbors

Sinclair Lewis of Sauk Center, Minnesota, and Thomas Wolfe of Asheville, North Carolina, are among the early-twentieth-century American writers who fled their small towns and then flayed them in fictional form—Lewis with *Main Street* and Wolfe with *Look Homeward, Angel*. The towns returned the snub by making each author persona non grata.

But torching your regional roots was not the era's only literary model. Consider the case of Zona Gale.

As an only child in Portage, Zona gazed at the wide Wisconsin River that flowed along Canal Street. In 1881, at age seven, she wrote her first story on wrapping paper and used a ribbon to bind the pages into a book. She read canonical works, including John Milton's *Paradise Lost* and John Bunyan's *The Pilgrim's Progress*, and recorded each plot in a notebook. Clearly Zona was an author in the making, and her parents supported her literary efforts—unusual for her time and place, not to mention her gender. With her mother's encouragement, she submitted a novel for publication at age thirteen and received the first of what would be many rejection letters.

Gale attended high school at the Wayland Academy in Beaver Dam and then entered the University of Wisconsin, where she achieved her first successes as a writer. She published in the college literary magazine and even placed a story in Milwaukee's *Evening Wisconsin*. When the newspaper mailed her first professional payment—a three-dollar check—she rode the train all the way from Madison to Portage to show it off to her parents.

After graduation, Gale headed straight for the *Evening Wisconsin* office, presenting herself to the editor every day for two weeks until he agreed to let her write another story. It was a trifling assignment—a report on a flower show—but Gale gave it everything she had. "I have never put so much emotion into anything else that I have written," she recalled.[1] Knowing a star when he saw one, the editor made a spot for her on staff.

The budding journalist took the same approach to breaking down doors in New York City. In 1901, she showed up at the *New York World* day after day with a list of stories she was prepared to write until the skeptical editors finally relented. She secured a staff job, impressed the Manhattan literati, and—after a few more rejection letters—published short stories in prominent magazines.

In 1904, Gale made a career move that would have baffled Sinclair Lewis and Thomas Wolfe. She returned to Portage for the rest of her life. The small-town setting became the wellspring of her fiction: the courthouse, post office, churches, bakeries, twilight bonfires, holidays, funerals, young lovers, town gossips, wise elders, and, of course, the life-giving river. *Birth, Miss Lulu Bett,* and other bestselling books inspired by Portage made Gale a leading practitioner of literary realism. She drew on her journalistic skills to examine the pleasures and pitfalls of provincial life, and particularly the obstacles to women's fulfillment.

The plight of one such thwarted heroine is the subject of *Miss Lulu Bett,* which Gale turned into a daringly true-to-life play that won a 1921 Pulitzer Prize in the drama category—the first ever awarded to a woman. Gale sat in the audience with her Portage friends when a touring production of *Miss Lulu Bett* opened in Madison later that year. Cheered by the crowd, the author went on stage to thank "the home folks and neighbors."[2]

Gale used the substantial earnings from her books' sales to build a Greek Revival–style house on Canal Street, with a study facing the beautiful Wisconsin River. She didn't hole up there, though—not with a raft of problems to solve in her city and state. Few writers have matched Gale in civic involvement. She spoke out for women's rights, racial equality, education, and pacifism, and she put her time and money where her mouth was. She served on the American Union Against Militarism, Wisconsin Free Library Commission, University of Wisconsin Board of Regents, Woman's Peace Party, and National Woman's Party, even helping draft the Wisconsin equal rights law in 1921. So greatly did she care about her hometown that she even advocated for saving a stately oak tree that was endangered by a new building.

Why would a rich, famous, critically acclaimed writer choose to spend her days in Portage? Gale put it simply: "I have my river."[3]

38

H. H. Bennett

Into the Wild

Henry Hamilton Bennett had no formal training in photography. He relied on homemade cameras, cobbled together with his carpentry know-how. He grew up living hand-to-mouth in the nineteenth-century frontier town of Kilbourn City (now known as Wisconsin Dells), far from the East Coast's cultural capitals. These were formidable obstacles for a photographer now enshrined in the Museum of Modern Art in New York, the Art Institute of Chicago, and the Getty Museum—and that's not even considering the Civil War injury that left him with only two working fingers on his right hand.

The disability forced twenty-five-year-old Bennett to abandon carpentry and take up the new medium of photography as a way of scraping by in Kilbourn City. With his adventurous spirit and love of nature, however, he had little interest in churning out portraits in the studio. It was excursions to his happy place—a wild stretch of the Wisconsin River known as the Dells—that awakened his inner artist.

Getting there was no easy task, especially with 1860s photographic equipment. Bennett tramped into caves, across cliffs, and through the mud with a bulky camera in his hands and a portable darkroom strapped to his back. He strove to transform the unruly terrain into orderly compositions, taking shot after shot of the river and the rock formations until they seemed perfectly picturesque. Sometimes, would-be customers joined him on these trips. Bennett rendered the stuffy Victorians as pictorial elements in nature, and he later sold them the prints, thus turning his refined scenes into souvenirs.

H. H. Bennett's 1886 "Leaping the Chasm," which pictured his son, Ashley, in mid-jump, boldly introduced the world to stop-action photography.
WHI IMAGE ID 2101

While Bennett had an artist's eye, he also had a struggling businessman's need to support his wife and children. He created silvery tableaux that tourists wanted to own, as well as promotional images that would attract even more tourists to the area. These included vast panoramas that hung in train stations and images that leaped into three dimensions when viewed through a handheld stereoscope. As his artwork circulated around the world, Bennett helped turn the Wisconsin Dells into a destination. Seen through his lens, the landscape achieved a mythic status that rivaled Ansel Adams's later views of Yosemite.

Bennett wore many hats throughout his lifetime: inventor, explorer, civic booster. His renowned 1886 photo titled "Leaping the Chasm," which features his son jumping from one towering rock to another, neatly encapsulates his achievements. It was a technological marvel that debuted stop-action photography, thanks to Bennett's invention of an instant-release shutter. It was an artistic triumph, counterposing the dramatic landscape with a dynamic human gesture. And with its vision of recreational activity in a sublime setting, it made everyone want to visit the Dells.

After establishing his reputation, Bennett suffered a series of setbacks. He lost his first wife, then he lost business starting in 1888 when Kodak produced an inexpensive camera that tourists could use themselves. In the 1890s, he launched a campaign to stop a dam project that would destroy parts of his beloved Dells. It was a doomed effort, and the dam's construction began shortly after his death in 1908, at age sixty-four.

In another way, however, Bennett won his last fight. Through his photographs, that pristine version of the Dells will never die.

39

Avi

"I Fooled You"

Edward Wortis entered the University of Wisconsin in 1955 after a lifetime's struggle with dysgraphia, a neurological disorder that impairs the ability to write. It's not that Wortis had trouble coming up with ideas; it's that he had trouble getting words down on paper. Ever since elementary school, teachers had thrown up their hands at his spelling errors, ungrammatical sentences, and illegible handwriting.

But Wortis yearned for a literary career. He majored in history and theater with the goal of becoming a playwright. That led him to a UW playwriting contest and an embarrassment he never forgot. "The professor who judged the contest wrote a comment on my manuscript," he told me in 2021. "It said, 'This is not a very good play, but the author is to be congratulated. He is clearly not a native English speaker and is making good progress with the English language.'"[1]

That insult would have discouraged a lesser artist, but not Wortis. He entered the playwriting contest the next year and, amazingly, won. After earning a UW master's degree in theater, he switched genres to become a children's novelist—one who now ranks among the greatest of our time. Under the pen name Avi, he has written more than eighty bestselling books and earned top honors in the field, including a Newbery Medal for *Crispin: The Cross of Lead* and Newbery Honors for *The True Confessions of Charlotte Doyle* and *Nothing but the Truth*.

The UW playwriting contest contributed to his success, providing a hint that Wortis might have what it took to be a writer. Another hint? The fact that his brain overflowed with characters to create, settings to explore, and stories to tell.

Avi grew up in New York City with writing in his blood. An aunt and three grandparents had been writers, so it seemed like an achievable goal—unlike, say, becoming a baseball player, his other childhood dream. Along with reading, he avidly followed 1940s radio serials, which offered a daily tutorial in storytelling.

Upon graduating from the UW, Avi labored at playwriting in San Francisco and New York City with little success. His fortunes changed when he began making up stories for his three-year-old son. He turned those bedtime tales into his first published book, 1970's *Things That Sometimes Happen*, after which his imagination kicked into overdrive.

Avi's steady stream of novels displayed an impressive range of subject matter and settings. *The True Confessions of Charlotte Doyle* is about an 1830s sea voyage, while *Crispin: The Cross of Lead* follows a wrongly accused peasant in medieval England. Other books delve into the Revolutionary War, World War II–era Brooklyn, and Renaissance Italy. Following the model of his favorite 1940s radio programs, he immerses readers in a series of artfully detailed worlds.

After a half-century in the business, Avi still struggles with the act of writing. In our interview, he surprised me with the fact that he revises manuscripts seventy to eighty times before they're finished—a habit rooted in his dysgraphia. It's a process that harks back to the days when he would try, over and over, to correct his error-ridden papers for school.

I noted that his finished novels show no signs of such anguish, seeming to flow effortlessly from the author's pen.

"Well," he said dryly, "I fooled you."

Scene Stealers

40

Chris Farley

Commitment to the Gag

In the 1980s, I lived in downtown Madison near a garage that had been converted into a closet-sized theater. Chris Farley performed there with the sketch-comedy troupe Ark Improv, but the place seemed way too small for him. He was a big guy with a big personality, inclined to slam into walls and props.

Chris grew up in Madison in a devout Catholic family, spending his teenage summers in the 1970s as a camp counselor near Minocqua. He often impressed friends with his kindness, but he also had a wild side, which led to substance abuse during his college years at Milwaukee's Marquette University.

Farley moved back to Madison in 1986 and worked for his dad's oil company, where he specialized in making customers laugh. One desperate night, he turned up at Ark Improv's door in a drunken stupor, asking about an audition. He needed a direction—an outlet for his impulses that had no place in business or church. Could comedy be his salvation?

Chris soon wrangled an audition. With all eyes on him, and his future on the line, he fell violently out of a chair. Alarmed troupe members thought he'd had a heart attack until they realized he was joking. Impressed by his commitment to the gag, they hired him on the spot.

So began Farley's career of busting up the stage. In addition to his loud physical humor, it became apparent that he could bring out a character's quiet side. Clearly, Ark's one-hundred-seat theater could not hold him for long. He moved on to the major Chicago troupes ImprovOlympic and Second City, and in 1990, he ascended

For Chris Farley, pictured in 1996's *Black Sheep*, comedy was salvation.
WISCONSIN CENTER FOR FILM AND THEATER RESEARCH

to comedy heaven as a cast member on NBC's *Saturday Night Live*. The show's cohort of young performers—Adam Sandler, David Spade, Chris Rock, Julia Sweeney, Tim Meadows—realized they couldn't top him. Indeed, they could barely keep a straight face during their scenes with Farley, never knowing what he'd do next.

His characters quickly entered the national conversation: the overweight Chippendales dancer, the overeating Gap girl, and the Chicago Bears superfan who suffers a red-faced choking fit in his chair, recalling that startling Ark Improv audition. His bellowing motivational speaker ("I live in a *van* down by the *river!*") had also appeared in embryonic form at Ark.

As much as I loved seeing Farley fall onto coffee tables, reducing them to splinters, my favorite SNL routine was the subtler "Chris Farley Show." Tapping into his real-life sweetness, he plays a self-loathing simpleton who has somehow landed his own celebrity talk show. His flop sweat and foolish questions are hilarious, yes, but also a little heartbreaking. You don't expect such vulnerability in a sketch-comedy character.

Farley had five great years on *Saturday Night Live* and three hit movies, including the much-loved *Tommy Boy*. Then, as periodically happened, his wild side reemerged. He died in 1997 during a drug and alcohol binge, despite his repeated attempts at rehab.

Showbiz stars traveled to Madison for his funeral at Our Lady Queen of Peace Church. Sandler later wrote a song about the mournful experience, confessing that "nothing was harder than saying goodbye / Except watching Chris's father have his turn to cry."[1]

Farley was laid to rest in a modest chapel near Queen of Peace. It's down the street from where I live now, and I occasionally wander in to pay my respects. Like Ark Improv's converted garage, the place feels way too small for him.

41

Oprah Winfrey
The Best Christmas

Before achieving television stardom, Oprah Winfrey suffered what she described as a wretched childhood in Milwaukee, marred by poverty and abuse. And yet, at age twelve, she experienced her "best Christmas" at an apartment on North Tenth Street: a miraculous event that set her on a path toward healing.

Oprah grew up in rural Mississippi wearing dresses made out of potato sacks and moved to Milwaukee at age six to live with her mother, Vernita, who barely made ends meet as a housemaid. She endured rape, teen pregnancy, a miscarriage, and thoughts of suicide.

During this nightmarish period, Oprah had her transformative Christmas. It started on a dismal note in 1966 when her mother, having no money for presents, canceled the family celebration. "That's when I realized there was no Santa Claus," Winfrey said during a 2003 episode of her television show. " 'Cuz now he ain't comin' because we're *poor*?"[1]

Just as despair set in, three nuns on a charitable mission knocked on the apartment door. They handed out toys to Oprah and her siblings and also provided a turkey for Christmas dinner. "That was the best Christmas of my life because somebody remembered," she said, "and I wasn't going to have to be the kid that said I got nothing."

The memory stuck with Oprah as she turned her life around in high school. After being sent to live with her father in Nashville, she earned good grades, worked at a radio station, and won a college scholarship. At age nineteen, she shone as Nashville's first African

American TV news anchor. She was off and running, and in 1986 her self-titled daytime talk show began airing nationally. With a down-to-earth persona and a dedication to personal growth, Winfrey ascended to the celebrity A-list: producer, author, actress, and publisher.

Winfrey's Milwaukee Christmas directly inspired her philanthropy, including a 2002 South African initiative she called Christmas Kindness. With dozens of staff members, she traveled around the country delivering fifty thousand presents to orphaned and impoverished young people. Rather than writing a check, she arranged to personally hand gifts to children with their names attached. "I wanted to be able to look in each kid's face and say to that child, 'Somebody remembered you,'" she explained.

Winfrey described it as the most rewarding experience of her life, for deeply personal reasons. "It was my mission," she said, "to do for them what the nuns had done for me."

And so does one kind act in 1966 Milwaukee echo through the ages.

42

Meinhardt Raabe

A Perfect Coroner

Meinhardt Raabe appeared in only one movie—1939's *The Wizard of Oz*—and only for thirteen seconds. But as the coroner of Munchkinland, sharing the screen with Judy Garland, Raabe makes an impression. It was enough to ensure him a seven-decade career that included major-media interviews, TV appearances, documentaries, an autobiography, speaking engagements, festival and convention showcases, mountains of fan mail, and a star on the Hollywood Walk of Fame. When he died in 2010, obituaries ran in the *New York Times, Los Angeles Times*, the BBC, and *Variety*. And all for those few unforgettable seconds of screen time.

Meinhardt was born in 1915 to a farm family in Farmington, not unlike Dorothy Gale's in *The Wizard of Oz*. During his teenage years at Johnson Creek High School, he was about three and a half feet tall—and, with no idea that other little people existed, imagined himself unique in all the world. That changed on a trip to the 1933 Chicago World's Fair, which featured little people as performers. In 1934, he found work there as a barker and announcer to help put himself through school at Watertown's Northwestern College. "This was the first time in my life that I actually witnessed little people, with friends their own size, falling in love, marrying, and raising families," he said.[1]

Raabe experienced his share of ridicule, but he had guts and ambition and didn't let it slow him down. He transferred to the University of Wisconsin and graduated with a business degree in 1937. The Oscar Mayer corporation recognized his natural talents as a performer and hired him to play Little Oscar, "the world's smallest

In this 1939 *Wizard of Oz* publicity still, Meinhardt Raabe (third from left) brandishes proof that the Wicked Witch of the East is "really most sincerely dead." WISCONSIN CENTER FOR FILM AND THEATER RESEARCH

chef," promoting its products in the hot-dog-shaped Weinermobile. Ever adventurous, Raabe requested time off in 1938 when Metro-Goldwyn-Mayer Studios put out a call for little people to appear in a certain movie.

The studio hired more than a hundred actors to play Munchkins in *The Wizard of Oz* and needed nine for speaking parts. Raabe's casting as the coroner was no fluke. He'd developed an exuberant stage presence at Oscar Mayer and the World's Fair, working especially hard on diction. "I had done a considerable amount of public speaking which started by winning a declamatory contest in which I had to speak as loudly and forcefully as possible," he said. "After that I went on to study phonics, learning to pronounce each syllable clearly."[2]

Raabe's scene represents a turning point in Dorothy's Technicolor journey of self-discovery. Her flying Kansas farmhouse has flattened the Wicked Witch of the East, and she'll earn heroic status if the Munchkins can confirm the villain's death. Though illogical in the extreme, *The Wizard of Oz* obsesses on standards of proof: Dorothy requires a broom to prove the Wicked Witch of the West's defeat, and her fellow outcasts need trinkets to show they have brains, heart, and courage.

In Munchkinland, proof falls to Raabe's character. Fitted out in a pointy beard and purple scrolled hat, he could have seemed simply ridiculous. But Raabe lends the character a stately presence as he unfurls the all-important death certificate, reciting lines as famous as any by Humphrey Bogart: "As coroner, I must aver / I thoroughly examined her. / And she's not only merely dead, / She's really most sincerely dead!" With that one moment of glory, the game Wisconsin actor secured himself a place in movie history.

He also gained a measure of star power. Raabe stood next to Garland in a prominent *Wizard of Oz* publicity still, brandishing the official-looking Certificate of Death. In August 1939, he returned to Watertown as a special guest for the film's premiere at the Classic Theater on Main Street. Then he traded his coroner's costume for a military uniform, obtaining his pilot's license in the Civil Air Patrol during World War II.

Throughout his life, Raabe maintained a connection to the Watertown area. He donated generously to the Bethesda Lutheran Home to support people with developmental disabilities, understanding the discrimination they faced. As a local celebrity, he spoke with the *Watertown Daily Times* whenever he passed through town.

Until the end of his life, Raabe held onto a treasured possession: a photograph signed for him by his costar. "For Meinhardt," Judy Garland wrote. "A perfect coroner, and person, too."[3]

43

Charlie Hill

Speaking His Truth

On October 20, 1977, TV audiences witnessed a transitional moment in the history of American Indian representation in the mainstream media. Charlie Hill performed a standup routine on NBC's *Richard Pryor Show*, becoming the first Indigenous comedian to appear on national television. In the space of five minutes, Hill forced viewers to rethink four hundred years' worth of stereotypes and clichés.

In jeans and a red western shirt, Hill began in a genial tone. "I usually have trouble doing my act because I know a lot of you white people have never seen an Indian do standup comedy before. Like, for so long you probably thought Indians never had a sense of humor." Pause. "We never thought *you* were too funny, either!"

After getting a laugh with that sly nod to genocide, Hill riffed on ignorance. "People come up to me now and they say, 'Can you speak Indian?' And there are like, over three hundred tribes. You know, can you speak Indian, that's like, 'Can you speak Caucasian?'"

As he delivered these barbs, Hill's smile removed a bit of the sting—but only a bit. A joke about colonization, capped with an expert punchline, barely concealed his pain and anger. "That's the name they give us. 'Indians.' That's the name Columbus gave us, which is incorrect. He named us Indians because he thought he was in India, you know." Pause. "I'm sure glad he wasn't looking for *Turkey*!"

In the middle of this paradigm-shifting routine, Hill boldly declared his identity: "I'm Oneida. I'm from Wisconsin. It's part of the Iroquois Nation."[1]

Hill grew up on northern Wisconsin's Oneida Nation reservation, where his father—known for his sense of humor—served as vice chairman. Like a lot of kids in the 1960s, Charlie flipped through the odd miscellany available on three TV networks: sitcoms, westerns, talk shows, variety programs, cartoons. But he didn't just watch this stuff. He studied it.

The Jackie Gleason Show offered him a weekly clinic in comedy. Jack Paar's *Tonight Show* featured Dick Gregory telling sharp-edged political jokes. At age ten, Charlie watched in wonder as Gregory needled viewers for treating Native people even worse than they treated Black people. He vowed, then and there, to become a standup comedian himself. "I'm going to go for it," he thought. "I'm going to find a way. I'm going to learn how to do it."[2]

Hill attended high school in De Pere, majored in speech and drama at the University of Wisconsin–Madison, then worked as an actor in New York City and Seattle. He chose Los Angeles as the launching pad for his comedy career but bombed his first time onstage. Clearly, he realized, this vocation would require a methodical approach. Hill frequented open mics, took notes on other comedians, sought feedback, and cultivated his point of view. Finally, he secured an audition at LA's star-making Comedy Store.

Hill bonded with owner Mitzi Shore, a fellow UW–Madison alum who'd grown up in Green Bay, not far from the Oneida reservation. Unlike other comedy-club proprietors, Shore appreciated Hill's hard-hitting Native material and gave him creative freedom. Palling around with fellow Comedy Store newbies in search of a voice, including David Letterman, Robin Williams, and Michael Keaton, Hill honed his act to perfection.

He found a fan in Richard Pryor, who had a similar penchant for challenging mainstream values. When Hill received his invitation to Pryor's show, he planned to appear in sketches—until he got a look at the scripts. He balked at the demeaning material (for example, Pryor dressed as George Armstrong Custer with arrows in his back) and angled for a standup slot. For once, an American Indian would address a mass audience on his own terms, using comedy as both a truncheon and a teaching tool.

His performance that night bumped Hill to a new level, leading to appearances on *Roseanne, Moesha, The Tonight Show Starring Johnny Carson,* and *Late Night with David Letterman.* He died in 2013, at age sixty-two, though that wasn't the end of his story. On Hill's birthday in 2022, a new generation of fans discovered him in a featured Google logo illustration, which pictured the comedian clutching his microphone and speaking his truth.

Hill didn't hold back on criticizing America's colonialist history, but he also treasured his non-Native friends and supporters. He wanted people across cultures to laugh, not at Native people but with them. As he told one diverse crowd during an appearance at the Winnipeg Comedy Festival, "We're all welcome in the circle of humor here tonight. We're all related."[3]

44

Fred MacMurray

Dad with a Dark Side

Fred MacMurray was, basically, my dad.

Millions of my brothers and sisters in the Baby Boom generation looked up to him in the 1950s, '60s, and '70s, when he served as everybody's surrogate father in movies (*The Absent-Minded Professor, Son of Flubber, The Shaggy Dog*) and television (*My Three Sons*). The classic MacMurray character was decent and good-humored, much as MacMurray was reputed to be in real life. When asked about his acting technique, he usually gave the same answer: "I play myself."[1]

"I grew up in a small town," MacMurray said, referring to Beaver Dam. "You learn down-to-earth values in a small town—honesty, love, and the importance of the simple laws of nature."[2] His down-to-earth persona made him one of the twentieth century's biggest male stars, neck-and-neck with James Stewart and Henry Fonda (and a tier above Kenosha's Don Ameche and Racine's Fredric March). But there's one problem in slapping his career with a "family-friendly" label. When I grew old enough to watch the classic films *Double Indemnity* and *The Apartment*, I learned that my surrogate father had an unsavory side, one that didn't square with the image I'd long cherished.

MacMurray always emphasized the idyllic qualities of his Beaver Dam boyhood, including fishing, hunting, and high school sports. In reality, his traveling-musician father abandoned him at age five—a wound that never healed. Nevertheless, he followed in his dad's footsteps with a saxophone, playing gigs at a roadhouse on Beaver Dam Lake. He also performed with the band Tom Joy's

Gloom Chasers during his brief stint at Waukesha's Carroll College. Music paved the way for his unexpected detour into acting.

After a move west in 1928, MacMurray played the vaudeville circuit with a band called the California Collegians. When a theatrical revue needed a musician to come onstage for a throwaway line, all eyes turned to the tall, handsome saxophone player with wavy hair—the one the girls back in Beaver Dam had called a dreamboat. With shaking hands, Fred delivered his line and got noticed. Next came a screen test, a Hollywood contract, and some hastily arranged acting lessons on the Paramount lot. But the twenty-six-year-old barely needed them, proving to be a natural onscreen. Within a year, he was a hit with fans and critics and was paired with such top-rank actresses as Claudette Colbert (in *The Gilded Lily*), Katharine Hepburn (in *Alice Adams*), and Carole Lombard (in *Hands across the Table*). After a long run of box-office successes as a romantic lead in the 1930s and '40s, he had a second wind in middle age with dear-old-dad roles in Disney movies and on TV. The man could work sitcom magic on *My Three Sons* with nothing more than an artfully arched eyebrow.

According to Charles Tranberg's MacMurray biography, fame and fortune did not change him. Ever modest, he kept a level head, avoided the spotlight, and dodged passes from his lascivious costars. In 1937, the Paramount extras voted him their favorite actor due to his kindness on set. His wife, June Haver, said, "[He] lives like he would if he were still back in Beaver Dam, Wisconsin."[3]

The town remained a touchstone. MacMurray returned throughout his life and went fishing with old friends on Beaver Dam Lake. In 1941, he rode in the Beaver Dam centennial celebration, crowned the festival queen, and sang part of "On, Wisconsin" before forgetting the words. He even used Beaver Dam as his character's hometown in the 1945 comedy *Pardon My Past*. He once told a group of residents that they could knock on his door in Hollywood, say the words "Beaver Dam," and be treated like family.

It's ironic, then, that posterity will remember MacMurray for two roles that had the least to do with his Beaver Dam values. In

In the 1944 film noir masterpiece *Double Indemnity*, Fred MacMurray (left) daringly cast aside his wholesome image. WISCONSIN CENTER FOR FILM AND THEATER RESEARCH

each case, writer-director Billy Wilder talked him into playing against type over his initial objections. And in each case, Fred proved that, when given a chance, he could hold his own with any actor of the day.

In the 1944 film noir masterpiece *Double Indemnity*, he plays smart-aleck insurance agent Walter Neff, who's so infatuated with a seductive new client (Barbara Stanwyck) that he agrees to bump off her old man and scam his own company for the payout. The murder plot kicks into gear so quickly that a lesser actor might have struggled to make psychological sense of Walter's decision. But in his first scene with Stanwyck, MacMurray communicates everything we need to know about this chump-in-the-making: his venality, gullibility, and misplaced sense of superiority, not to mention a lustiness so raw it must have scandalized the neighbors back in

Wisconsin. If Fred truly did "play himself" onscreen, this was a part of him he'd never shown publicly.

The cynical 1960 comedy *The Apartment* gave him another chance to taint his nice-guy brand. As a corporate boss who conducts an adulterous affair in an underling's apartment, he's all smiles on the outside: the picture of respectability, à la *My Three Sons*. On the inside, though, it's pure rot. MacMurray puts a hard edge on his affable expression, hinting at depths of depravity in the American family man.

The Apartment was an Oscar-winning hit, but not everyone appreciated MacMurray's dramatic range. After the movie opened, a disillusioned woman accosted him on the street, hit him with her handbag, and shouted, "How could you?"[4]

It's a good question with no obvious answer. We can only be glad he did.

45

Harrison Ford

Han Solo in Williams Bay

A long time ago, in a galaxy far, far away from Hollywood, Harrison Ford cultivated his roguish reputation in Wisconsin. That persona came in handy for his 1977 breakthrough performance as Han Solo, the *Star Wars* smuggler who takes orders "from just one person: me!"

Ford entered Ripon College in 1960 as a C student from the Chicago suburbs. He had no particular academic goals and drifted for four years. He signed up for ROTC but left after refusing to cut his hair. He hustled at the pool hall and lost interest in his philosophy major. By his senior year, he had become thoroughly disrespectable, sleeping through his classes and nearly flunking out.

Then a miracle occurred in central Wisconsin. Ford signed up for a theater class during his last quarter. He conquered his stage fright, donned a fake mustache, and starred in *The Skin of Our Teeth* in Ripon's Red Barn Theater. By the end of the term, Harrison scarcely cared that he wouldn't graduate due to bad grades. He had found his calling, or so he thought.

That summer, he tested the waters with his first paid acting job in Williams Bay. The Wisconsin village had its own summer stock repertory company, the Belfry Players, which performed in a converted Mormon church. Ford's status as a resident actor required him to help out with carpentry—a small price to pay for the onstage experience.

At the start of the summer season, he drove to Milwaukee to marry his college girlfriend, Mary Marquardt. Rather than go on a honeymoon, they headed back to Williams Bay after the wedding so Harrison could perform that night in *Take Her, She's Mine*. Mary found work in the Belfry Players' box office, and the two lived together in a dormitory adjoining the theater.

Sporting a 1964 Beatles-style mop-top, Ford appeared in six plays. Despite occasionally flubbing his lines, he felt himself maturing as an actor. At the end of the summer, he and Mary packed up their old Volkswagen so Harrison could try his luck in Hollywood.

It took a while—and a few more carpentry gigs on the side— but he parlayed his devilish charisma into huge hits with the *Star Wars* and *Indiana Jones* series. By the 1980s, he had become not only a top-grossing action star, but also an Oscar-nominated actor for his dramatic role in *Witness*.

In 1985, Ford was offered a less glitzy recognition: an honorary degree from Ripon College, where he'd flunked out two decades earlier. But he turned the school down, once again dodging respectability in the state of Wisconsin. A gesture truly worthy of Han Solo.

46

Agnes Moorehead

Citizen Kane's Mother

At age nineteen, Agnes Moorehead moved with her family from Ohio to Wisconsin. Her father served as pastor of Reedsburg's First Presbyterian Church, with her mother acting as organist and choir director. In the mid-1920s, Moorehead spent five years teaching English and public speaking in Soldiers Grove, but a photograph from the era—in which she lowers her chin, purses her lips, and fixes the lens with the smoldering black-rimmed eyes of a silent movie star—suggests she wasn't long for the local high school.

In 1927, Moorehead headed to the American Academy of Dramatic Arts in New York City to pursue her calling as an actor. After a few lean years, she joined Orson Welles's Mercury Theatre and excelled as a stage and radio performer. She moved to Hollywood in 1939 and just three years later earned an Academy Award nomination for her role in Welles's *The Magnificent Ambersons*—the first of four Oscar nods in her career, along with two wins at the Golden Globes and one at the Emmys. Though usually a supporting player, she made the most of her time on camera in *Dark Passage; Hush ... Hush, Sweet Charlotte*; and other films and TV shows that continue to find an audience. As a cast of one in "The Invaders," a memorable episode of *The Twilight Zone*, she holds the screen without a word of dialogue. On the ABC hit series *Bewitched*, she steals every scene she's in as Endora, an imperious witch casting spells on the son-in-law she despises.

Moorehead retained her ties to Reedsburg, regularly returning to visit family. In 1971, she spoke at the dedication of a new city hall complex and admitted to "a feeling of nostalgia" for Wisconsin.[1] She

Agnes Moorehead's soulful intensity earned her a key role in the greatest movie ever made. WISCONSIN CENTER FOR FILM AND THEATER RESEARCH

even left her papers to the University of Wisconsin, having attended summer school there for library and teaching courses.

These connections allow Wisconsin to claim one of the country's best actors as its own. Of all Moorehead's roles, the one most likely to guarantee her immortality is a brief turn in 1941's *Citizen Kane*, the Welles film that's often considered cinema's greatest achievement.

Snow falls outside a modest boarding house. Young Charles Foster Kane stands by his Rosebud sled, throwing snowballs. The camera pulls back until an imposing figure enters the frame: Charles's mother, Mary (Moorehead), who tenderly calls to him from the window.

Mary has come into money and believes that sending Charles away from home is in his best interest. We see from her son's tears—in a wrenching closeup—that she is mistaken. The wound will never heal, even when Charles becomes a powerful newspaper tycoon. It's no wonder his dying word is "Rosebud."

Welles suffered a similar trauma during his own Wisconsin childhood, so you can bet he thought long and hard about whom to cast as the wonderful/terrible mother. In her few minutes on screen, Moorehead conveys Mary's mixed emotions with a gulp, a sigh, and an almost imperceptible quiver in her voice. The portrayal is all the more moving for the actor's restraint.

Midway through the scene, as Mary again gazes out the window, we get our first good look at Moorehead's eyes—soulful and intense, recalling that long-ago photograph from Soldiers Grove.

47

Hattie McDaniel

A Springboard to Hollywood

You may despise 1939's *Gone with the Wind* for romanticizing slavery. And you may despise the movie's Mammy character for promoting the racist stereotype of an enslaved person who gratefully serves her enslavers. But Hattie McDaniel, who brought humor and humanity to this problematic role, deserves a more tolerant response.

McDaniel broke barriers in Hollywood at a time when doing so often required compromise. Again and again, she played the role of a servant because Black actors had few other choices. With persistence and skill, however, McDaniel distinguished herself in show business. She became the first Black actor to win an Academy Award, for *Gone with the Wind*; the first Black actor to star in her own radio show, in 1947; and the first Black Oscar winner to be pictured on a US postage stamp, in 2006. Her efforts initiated the process that led from Lena Horne to Sidney Poitier to Halle Berry to #OscarsSoWhite—in other words, the slow but ongoing process of reform.

Hattie's parents had been born into slavery, and she grew up poor in Denver. But from an early age, she displayed a never-say-die spirit that earned her the nickname "The Old Pep Machine." Young Hattie sang, danced, acted, and wrote blues music during the 1920s while supporting herself as a cook and a maid. A turning point came in January 1930, when she visited Milwaukee in a touring production of *Show Boat*.

The stock market had recently crashed, and the tour was struggling. McDaniel lost her job and found herself broke and stranded.

"Somebody told me of a place as a maid in the ladies' room at Sam Pick's Suburban Inn," she wrote in a 1947 article for *The Hollywood Reporter*. "I rushed out there and took the job."[1]

McDaniel toiled for a dollar a day at the Suburban Inn out on Bluemound Road, hoping for a chance to perform in the club's floor show. Late one night, after all the entertainers left, the manager needed a volunteer to go on stage. The Old Pep Machine stepped forward with a powerhouse rendition of "The St. Louis Blues," and a Milwaukee star was born.

McDaniel became a Suburban Inn headliner, attracting huge crowds. Her local fans kept asking why she didn't go to Hollywood, and after a couple of years, she asked herself the same question. She boarded a bus to Los Angeles with twenty dollars in her purse and found work as an extra. Soon came bigger parts, the 1940 Academy Award for Best Supporting Actress, and a hit radio and TV show called *Beulah* that ran through 1954. "Milwaukee was really my springboard to Hollywood," McDaniel said.[2]

Some critics knocked her for playing undignified roles, even though she valiantly fought discrimination and supported racial justice issues like fair housing. But McDaniel remained a scrapper and a survivor and had no trouble standing up for herself. "I have struggled for eleven years to open up opportunities for our group in the industry," she said in 1942, "and have tried to reflect credit upon my race, in exemplary conduct both on- and off-screen."[3]

The real-life role Hattie McDaniel played in the movie industry was anything but undignified. As future generations cringe at *Gone with the Wind*, they can at least look back fondly at her barrier-breaking ways.

48

Rodney Dangerfield

A Slob among the Snobs

For a midsized city tucked away in the heartland, Madison has served as the location for a surprising number of major movies. Most of them feature big stars in their most forgettable roles. What is it about filming in Wisconsin's capital city that brought out the worst in Julia Roberts and Nick Nolte (*I Love Trouble*), Christian Bale and Billy Crudup (*Public Enemies*), Keanu Reeves and Morgan Freeman (*Chain Reaction*), Zach Braff and Rachel Bilson (*The Last Kiss*), and Molly Ringwald (*For Keeps*)?

Though it's hard to believe, the best performance filmed in Madison came from an actor who was never even briefly considered for an Academy Award. The 1986 hit *Back to School* stars Rodney Dangerfield as vulgar businessman Thornton Melon, who joins his son Jason (Keith Gordon) as the world's unlikeliest freshman at Grand Lakes University—in real life, the University of Wisconsin–Madison.

Thornton is a self-made millionaire who believes strongly in education even though he's barely seen the inside of a classroom. Concerned about Jason's social struggles at college, he shows up to serve as a role model for living large. He wisecracks his way through iconic UW settings, bribes the school's president (Ned Beatty), pays Kurt Vonnegut to write him a paper on the subject of Kurt Vonnegut, woos a soulful English professor (Sally Kellerman), and violates every known NCAA rule in an extravagantly silly finale with the campus diving team.

Thornton offends everyone and everything, to the point where the film itself is sometimes offensive. Though some of the attitudes

Rodney Dangerfield filmed *Back to School* on the UW–Madison campus in 1985, creating a character both tacky and touching.
UNIVERSITY OF WISCONSIN–MADISON ARCHIVES

are outdated, Dangerfield's performance stands the test of time. He positions himself on the crass end of twentieth-century Jewish comedy, combining the verbal wit of Groucho Marx, the physical inventiveness of Curly Howard, and the funny faces of Jerry Lewis. Dangerfield brings his own twitchy, eye-popping, head-bobbing style to the mix, incorporating snappy one-liners from his standup act. "The football team at my high school, they were *tough*," he barks, assuming his "I don't get no respect" persona. "After they sacked the quarterback, they went after his *family*!"

Following *Caddyshack* and *Easy Money*, *Back to School* offered nothing new in casting the comedian as a slob among the snobs. But filming in sincere Wisconsin rather than cynical LA brought out a different side of Dangerfield. Here, he comes off as practically poignant. Thornton's tenderness toward his son gives the ridiculous premise a whiff of credibility. His rapport with the professor gives the love story an eccentric charm. And his third-act dedication to passing his courses at Grand Lakes gives the normally sarcastic Rodney Dangerfield the rare chance to touch a movie audience.

Near the end of the film, Thornton intones Dylan Thomas's "Do Not Go Gentle into That Good Night," followed by an impassioned statement of purpose: "I'm stayin' in school!" He scrapes by with Ds, but never have mediocre grades been so inspiring.

49

Allen Ludden

The Password Is . . .

On a 2022 visit to Mineral Point to take in the historic mining sites and nineteenth-century architecture, I stumbled onto a bit of local lore I'd known nothing about. I overheard a conversation about Allen Ludden, the smooth-talking TV game-show host of the 1960s and '70s. And at the Red Rooster Cafe, my paper placemat listed Ludden's grave as a Mineral Point highlight. Many people might have shrugged and continued touring the art galleries on High Street. But not me.

I grew up watching Ludden's *Password*, in which contestants traded clues to guess a mystery word. Thrillingly, the word was confided to the TV audience with a whispery voiceover that only we could hear: "The password is . . . ." As an elementary-school bookworm, I appreciated a game-show host who glorified the English language. We even wore identical horn-rimmed glasses, though his made him look dashingly brainy and mine made me look like the last one you'd pick for dodgeball. While my friends watched cowboy shows, I kept the dial tuned to *Password* and—no surprise— grew up to be a writer rather than a ranch hand. I'd never thought about it before, but some of the credit was due to Allen Ludden.

After a hearty Welsh breakfast at the Red Rooster, I searched the internet for clues about Ludden's Mineral Point connection. He was born there in 1917, and his father—an ice dealer—died just two years later of the Spanish flu. When Allen was five, his mother married the manager of the Mineral Point electrical plant, after which the family moved from Janesville to Elkhorn to Antigo to Waupaca. Allen attended college at the University of Texas, graduated Phi

Beta Kappa, and stayed on for grad school, earning a master's in English. Apparently, his intellectual image was no act.

After receiving a Bronze Star in World War II, Ludden hosted radio and television shows and found his star vehicle at *Password* in 1961. That's also where he met fellow TV personality Betty White. They fell in love, married, and worked together on stage and screen until Allen's death from cancer in 1981. White never remarried, saying, "Once you've had the best, who needs the rest?"[1]

Mineral Point became Ludden's final resting place, and townsfolk speculated that his dear Betty might be buried beside him. To their dismay, she chose to spend eternity somewhere other than southwestern Wisconsin, though she did donate Allen's papers to the Mineral Point library before her own death in 2021. Not a bad consolation prize.

My Allen Ludden journey ended with a pilgrimage to his gravesite on the western edge of town. To its credit, humble Graceland Cemetery gives no special treatment to Mineral Point's famous son. So, in the absence of signage, I wandered for a while through the sloping grounds. Finally, I found Ludden's tombstone, which mentions his service in World War II but nothing of his showbiz career. Indeed, the plot feels as far from his star on the Hollywood Walk of Fame as you can imagine, bordered by the Iowa County Fairgrounds and rolling farmers' fields.

The password is . . . *peaceful.*

50

Gena Rowlands

Raw Truth on the Screen

Gena Rowlands was born in Cambria in 1930, a descendant of the village's original Welsh settlers. Though it had only six hundred residents in the 1940s, Cambria cared about culture. The village funded a lavish library and hosted a Shakespeare club. Rowlands's mother often traveled to Madison to perform in plays. So it's no surprise that young Gena dreamed of an acting career herself.

She saw several movies a week and idolized tough gal Bette Davis. At eleven, she met movie star Fred MacMurray in nearby Beaver Dam, his hometown. If MacMurray could make the leap from southern Wisconsin to major motion pictures, why couldn't she? Rowlands began her acting career at fourteen, winning a three-year scholarship to the Jarvis Repertory Theater in Washington, DC. Then, it was back to her home state.

After entering the University of Wisconsin in 1947, she was selected as a "Badger Beauty" and featured prominently in the student yearbook. On the advice of a UW counselor, she left Madison in 1950 for the American Academy of Dramatic Arts in New York City—and her timing couldn't have been better.

It was a golden age for theater, movies, and live television, and Rowlands had the skills. She found work on Broadway, in Hollywood, and on TV anthology series such as *General Electric Theater* and *Studio One*. Even in conventional roles, she conveyed unconventional intensity.

Rowlands's 1954 marriage to John Cassavetes, a fellow student at the American Academy of Dramatic Arts, began a three-decade collaboration that would transform American film. As an actor, writer, and director, Cassavetes sought to move beyond dramatic clichés and put raw truth on the screen. In his influential indie movies, often with Rowlands in the lead, he gave actors the latitude to explore dark, dangerous corners of the human psyche. *Shadows, Faces*, and other now-classic Cassavetes works were financed by mainstream acting jobs and shot in the couple's home, with their friends and family as cast members. These were films made for love, not money.

The best Cassavetes/Rowlands production is 1974's *A Woman Under the Influence*. We meet Mabel (Rowlands) in motion. Preparing for a date with her husband (Peter Falk), she packs off the kids, paces from room to room, smokes, sings, whistles, mutters. Cassavetes's tracking camera can barely keep up with her—until date night falls apart and an ominous stillness sets in.

Mabel veers between manic and depressive, struggling to live up to the constricting roles of wife and mother. Rowlands delivers one of the best mad acts of the 1970s, up there with Peter Finch in *Network* and Robert De Niro in *Taxi Driver*. Even Mabel's indulgent spouse admits, "I don't understand what she's doing."

Viewers don't understand her, either. It's like trying to make sense of Ophelia's Act IV raving in *Hamlet*. Nevertheless, you can't take your eyes off Mabel. Her expressions—teeth bared, nostrils flaring—speak volumes about her troubled marriage. Even in a movie with virtually no plot, the actress keeps you on the edge of your seat. You never know what she'll do next.

Rowlands earned an Academy Award nomination for *A Woman Under the Influence*. On Oscar night in April 1975, she received a delivery of roses from her biggest fans: the folks back home in Cambria.

51

Harry Houdini

The Self-Liberator

My love affair with Harry Houdini began in second grade. I was staying at my grandparents' house when a St. Louis TV station aired a Saturday matinee of the 1953 *Houdini* biopic starring Tony Curtis. I watched, stunned, as the invincible magician broke out of strait-jackets and safes. He even broke out of a crate that had been wrapped in chains and dropped into a freezing river. "Nothing that man ever made," he announces, "can keep Houdini a prisoner!"

This guy wasn't a made-up character, according to my grand-father. He was an ordinary person, like me, who had learned to free himself from any restraint. I vowed, then and there, to pursue this line of work when I grew up.

I found a biography in my school library, tantalizingly called *The Man Who Walked through Walls*. I learned that Houdini was born Ehrich Weiss in Hungary in 1874 and then moved to Appleton, where his father served as the town rabbi. After struggling with dreary factory work in Milwaukee, he joined a circus and began devising his escape tricks. These became more elaborate as he rose to worldwide stardom, culminating in water-torture cells and even coffins.

Houdini's escapes involved real dexterity but also a fair amount of deceit. Rather than quickly breaking out of a safe, for example, he preferred to make the audience wait. That way, they'd gasp even louder when he finally emerged, triumphant.

As I got older—and more prudent—I lost interest in pursuing the escape-artist trade. But Houdini stuck with me as a metaphor. As an immigrant, he escaped not only from handcuffs but also from

Harry Houdini learned to free himself from any restraint, inspiring other beleaguered immigrants. WISCONSIN CENTER FOR FILM AND THEATER RESEARCH

poverty and oppression, becoming an inspiration for the downtrodden members of his audience. He called himself a self-liberator, and that's just what I aimed to be. I wanted to break free from any constraint that life threw at me.

When I moved to Wisconsin in the 1980s, I immediately planned a trip to Appleton. Here was my chance to make contact with Houdini, who'd regarded Appleton as his hometown and loved returning for performances. I spent a day walking in his footsteps, ogling his stage equipment at the local history museum, and communing with his spirit.

There's one other way to make contact with Houdini, and that's to seek out his actual spirit. To cap his career, the self-liberator planned to escape from death itself. Near the end of his life, he announced that he would reappear in ghostly form if he could only find a way. As a result, fans have held séances ever since he left our sphere in 1926. These are conducted on the day he died, Halloween.

He has yet to materialize, but I continue to hold out hope. After all, Houdini always knew the theatrical value of making us wait.

52

Carrie Coon

An Impractical Career

In 2003, Carrie Coon enrolled in acting school at the University of Wisconsin–Madison on a lark. She grew up as a sensible Ohio farmgirl in a big family that had no interest in plays. But she got a few parts in high school and in college at the University of Mount Union, where a professor suggested she apply to graduate programs in theater. When Coon arrived in Madison, she felt sheepish about pursuing such an "impractical" career.[1]

But the actor's life suited her. Plays by George Bernard Shaw and Tony Kushner sparked her imagination, and the rigorous rehearsals indulged her workaholic tendencies. Coon won fans with her intuitive approach to characters, and she soon branched out beyond university productions. She took on major parts at Madison Repertory Theatre, American Players Theatre in Spring Green, and Renaissance Theatreworks in Milwaukee. I was lucky enough to see her lead performance in 2007's *Anna Christie* at the Madison Rep, and I sensed (though it took no special critical genius) that the impassioned young performer was going places.

Coon continued to appear in Wisconsin productions after graduate school, doing voiceovers and training-video work to support herself. A move to Chicago finally set the star-making machinery in motion. Steppenwolf Theatre's 2010 production of *Who's Afraid of Virginia Woolf?* moved to Broadway and earned Coon a Tony nomination for her portrayal of Honey, the frustrated faculty wife. Next came a plum TV role in HBO's *The Leftovers* and her auspicious film debut in *Gone Girl*.

In this 2014 blockbuster, Margo (Coon) and Nick (Ben Affleck) are snide twins with a taste for board games. Game playing of a deadlier sort begins when Nick's wife (Rosamund Pike) goes missing under mysterious circumstances. Affleck and Pike fail to make sense of their characters' relationship, which wobbles between love and hate to satisfy the demands of an improbable cat-and-mouse story. The one actor who emerges with her dignity intact is Coon, who draws on her UW theatrical training to create a consistent character.

Though Margo is written as a contrivance, arriving on cue to deliver or react to new information, Coon brings so much more to the role. In a movie where neither of the main characters warrants our sympathy, she's the stalwart sister anybody would want during a murder investigation/media circus/con game. She takes her character beyond sarcasm to authentic desperation and despair. She even makes an emotional connection with Affleck—no mean feat given his determination to smirk through every plot twist.

Coon considered her *Gone Girl* performance a rookie effort, but it served as a prelude to her celebrated roles in *Fargo, Mary Jane, The Gilded Age*, and *Bug*: a sign of triumphs to come. Who says an acting career is impractical?

53

Willem Dafoe

The Appleton Work Ethic

Willem Dafoe was a young actor in a hurry. In 1973, he left his hometown of Appleton before finishing high school, bound for a theater program at the University of Wisconsin–Milwaukee. Then he left Milwaukee before finishing college, with his eye on the New York City drama scene. Though Wisconsin felt too small for his ambitions, the state set the course for his eventual career as a movie actor who's up for anything, from popular entertainment to unpopular experiments. Fans might be surprised to learn that the idiosyncratic characters he's played—Vincent Van Gogh, Jesus, the Green Goblin—have their roots in Appleton's Attic Theatre.

Dafoe was born in 1955 to career-oriented parents—his father a surgeon, his mother a nurse—and he absorbed their Midwestern discipline. As the second-youngest child of eight in a bustling household, he learned to get attention first by acting out, then simply by acting. The kid given to pranks and gags channeled his look-at-me energy into community theater. And the locals who attended Attic Theatre's *A Thousand Clowns* noticed something special. "Despite his age, 13, Bill does more than memorize lines and recite them at the proper time," wrote a perceptive critic for the *Appleton Post-Crescent* in 1969. "He actually ACTS and reacts and works subtleties into the part. His embellishments, surprisingly for a youth, are not just hamming it up. This is a lad with a promising future on the stage."[1]

As a teen, Dafoe sampled the 1960s counterculture during visits to Madison to see his older sisters at the University of Wisconsin. That only encouraged his transgressive streak, and at age seventeen,

Appleton East High School kicked him out (unfairly, he insists) for making what teachers considered a pornographic film. But no matter—the budding actor was already eager for something new. "I just knew there was another world out there," he later said, "and I wanted to find it."[2]

After finishing his high school requirements at Appleton's Lawrence University, Dafoe headed to the UW–Milwaukee theater department, which had impressed him with an intense production of *One Flew Over the Cuckoo's Nest*. He spent 1973 and '74 learning the ropes, awestruck by the talented teachers and students. Aside from working two jobs to fund his education, he ate, breathed, and slept theater—literally, in the case of sleeping. While immersed in productions of *Phaedra* and *A Moon for the Misbegotten*, he bedded down on a theater department couch rather than go home to his apartment on Farwell Avenue.

Still suffering from what he called "ants in my pants," Dafoe left the university during his sophomore year to join the experimental Milwaukee troupe Theatre X.[3] This is where he cultivated his trademark fearlessness on the stage, exploring the limits of human experience. His goal: to discover truth by any means necessary and to communicate that truth to an audience. In *O Wow Nancy Drew*, he gave an over-the-top drag performance; in *The Wreck: A Romance*, he got so caught up in a knife-wielding scene that he accidentally stabbed himself. Dafoe took the Theatre X attitude with him to New York City stages, and then to the movies.

In a replay of his expulsion from high school, he was kicked off his first film production, 1980's *Heaven's Gate*. (His transgression: laughing on set.) But Hollywood came to appreciate that Appleton work ethic. He broke through with memorable turns as both villains (the counterfeiter Eric Masters in *To Live and Die in L.A.*) and heroes (Jesus Christ in *The Last Temptation of Christ*). He boldly threw himself into comedy (*Grand Budapest Hotel*), high-prestige drama (*Mississippi Burning*), low-prestige drama (*Body of Evidence*), action movies (*Speed 2*), horror (*Shadow of the Vampire*), comic-book blockbusters (*Spider-Man*), biopics (*At Eternity's Gate*), strange stuff (*Wild at Heart*), and voice work for animated features (*Finding Nemo*). Along the way, he picked up multiple Academy Award nominations and, more important, challenged himself and his audience. With his unusually expressive (and just flat-out unusual) face, he seems alive to everyone and everything onscreen. You sense that he's discovering his characters right before your eyes.

"I'm in it for the adventure, the experience, the need to learn something, because when you're turned on you're more available, more transparent," he told *MKE Lifestyle* in 2023. "That's something that started to develop during my Theatre X days."[4]

Dafoe's achievements have made his hometown proud. A *Post-Crescent* ad for *Platoon* in 1987 noted that the film starred "Appleton's own Willem Dafoe." In 2022, he returned to UW–Milwaukee to accept an honorary doctorate, calling his stint in the theater department "a very formative and positive experience."[5] That same year, he also acknowledged his roots while hosting *Saturday Night Live*. During his opening monologue, two cast members impersonating Appleton natives heckled him about expunging his Wisconsin accent. Dafoe countered: "I can still speak Wisconsin!"[6]

Given the state's profound influence on his life and career, it's a safe bet that he'll be speaking Wisconsin till the day he dies.

54

Spencer Tracy

Welcome Back to Ripon

In some of his best-loved movies, Spencer Tracy plays a genial curmudgeon: the put-upon patriarch of *Father of the Bride* and *Guess Who's Coming to Dinner*; the needling spouse of *Adam's Rib*; the gruff coach of *Pat and Mike*. In these and other roles, the middle-aged Tracy is about as dangerous as a comfortable cardigan sweater. By contrast, the real-life Tracy grew up in Milwaukee as a hyper-active hellion who seemed destined for failure until he stumbled on his true calling at Ripon College.

The Tracy family moved from house to house in Milwaukee, with Spencer attending a half-dozen high schools. None interested him, and even the tough nuns at St. John's Cathedral failed to beat any sense into him. But Spencer's father insisted that he attend college, so after stints as a lamplighter, an athletic-club towel boy, and a US Navy seaman, the twenty-one-year-old enrolled at Ripon in 1921, with scant expectations of success.

Laughably, the young man who hated studying planned to major in medicine. But he drifted toward theater, earning rave reviews in a production of *The Truth*. Finally, something clicked. Tracy forgot about becoming a doctor and, for the first time in his life, applied himself. He cofounded a campus acting company and showed a knack for mastering his lines.

After being voted his class's second most popular student, "Spence" left Ripon for a career on Broadway, and then in the movies. He won back-to-back Best Actor Oscars for 1937's *Captains Courageous* and 1938's *Boys Town*, branding himself as a decent, rugged, unpretentious paragon of American masculinity.

Spencer Tracy won an Oscar for his role in 1937's *Captains Courageous* shortly before his triumphant return to Ripon College for Spencer Tracy Day. WISCONSIN CENTER FOR FILM AND THEATER RESEARCH

Though now a box-office star and critical darling, he didn't forget Wisconsin.

On June 10, 1940, Ripon's Campus Theater premiered the film *Edison, The Man*, with the star in attendance for Spencer Tracy Day in Ripon. Tracy made a grand entrance in a twenty-five-car motorcade, escorted by a fleet of Milwaukee police officers on motorcycles. He brought along a suitably excessive entourage, including representatives from Metro-Goldwyn-Mayer Studios, who must have enjoyed seeing a real heartland town after fabricating so many of them for the movies.

The *Ripon Weekly Press* published a special fourteen-page edition called "Welcome Back, Spencer" that glorified the returning hero. And Tracy, the notoriously errant student, donned academic robes to receive an honorary degree from Ripon College. The degree was not in medicine, thank heavens, but in dramatic arts.

55

André De Shields

Roles of a Lifetime

André De Shields was born for the stage. Witness his commanding performance in Broadway's *The Wiz*, snapping his white cape while belting out "So You Wanted to See the Wizard." So it's disheartening to learn that racism once kept him out of University of Wisconsin theater productions.

In the 1960s, Madison was known for its antiwar protests, and De Shields yearned to join the revolution. In 1968, he transferred to the university from Wilmington College with the goal of changing the world through theater. At first, that plan ran into a brick wall. He auditioned for every campus production, impressed fellow students with his acting and singing, but made no headway with the theater faculty. Having grown up in segregated Baltimore, the Black actor was no stranger to prejudice, and the rejections stung.

So De Shields turned to unconventional off-campus productions and instantly found his niche. Screw Theater recognized his intensity and cast him in a version of *Titus Andronicus* in which the actors grunted like cavemen rather than speaking Shakespeare's dialogue. Later, he played Martha in Screw's gender-bending *Who's Afraid of Virginia Woolf?* Most memorably, he danced nude as Tiger Lily in a controversial antiwar adaptation of *Peter Pan*.

In 1969, De Shields learned of auditions for a Chicago production of *Hair*. He lacked funds for the ten-dollar round-trip bus ticket, but three women friends on campus loaned him the money—on the condition that he pay them back handsomely when he made it big. He wrote out a playful IOU to one of them: "I, the undersigned, do hereby promise, pledge, and swear to escort Miss Nina

Lepinsky on and finance a world-wind [*sic*], jet-set, leisurely tour of the planet Earth."[1]

De Shields slept overnight on a Chicago park bench and competed with hundreds of other hopefuls. He returned to Madison and, to his surprise, received a callback. After borrowing money for yet another bus ticket to Chicago, he won a part.

The rest is Broadway history. De Shields went on to star in the musicals *The Wiz, Play On!,* and *The Full Monty.* In 1982, he won an Emmy Award for Outstanding Individual Achievement for a broadcast of *Ain't Misbehavin'.* In 2019, his full-throated performance in *Hadestown* earned a Tony Award for Best Featured Actor in a Musical. In his Tony acceptance speech, De Shields thanked all the people "who have loved me into consciousness," surely thinking of those three UW friends who believed in him enough to pay for a couple of bus tickets.[2] He stayed in touch with them and, true to his word, treated them to "jet-set" nights on the town whenever they visited him in New York City.

At the end of his Tony speech, the actor offered a hard-won bit of wisdom: "The top of one mountain is the bottom of the next, so keep climbing." It's exhilarating to think of De Shields's experience at Screw Theater as the first peak in a series of summits. Who wouldn't want to follow him on that trip into the stratosphere?

56

Mary Hinkson

Cave of the Heart

In 1943, University of Wisconsin freshman Mary Hinkson arrived in Madison from Philadelphia, facing a Black student's infuriating quandary: where to live? Doors were closed at white-only dormitories and rooming houses. Hinkson could have taken a room at a segregated facility off-campus, but Groves Women's Cooperative offered a novel opportunity for diverse students to live together. So she moved into the integrated co-op—milestone number one in a life of breaking barriers.

Mary planned to study physical education but pirouetted to dance after a course with famed professor Margaret H'Doubler, who'd established the nation's first dance major at the UW in 1926. H'Doubler's unconventional methods—for example, instructing students to explore movements while lying blindfolded on the floor—encouraged Hinkson to pursue an individual style.

She joined the UW dance troupe Orchesis as a pioneering Black member, then obtained her UW master's degree and taught in the physical education department. That made her one of the first Black women instructors at any majority-white university.

But Hinkson's physicality transcended physical education. She cofounded the interracial Wisconsin Dance Group in the late 1940s and toured the Midwest before heading for the dance mecca of New York City. In 1951, modern-dance master Martha Graham recognized Hinkson's talent and accepted her into the previously all-white Martha Graham Dance Company. In Graham's *Diversion of Angels* ballet, Hinkson memorably partnered with Bertram Ross, a gay, white, Jewish man: an early example of an integrated dancing pair.

After an unconventional education at the University of Wisconsin, Mary Hinkson—pictured during a college performance in the mid-1940s—had no use for dance-world limitations. UNIVERSITY OF WISCONSIN-MADISON ARCHIVES

Hinkson starred in Graham's dances for more than two decades, owning the stage in *Circe* and *Cave of the Heart*. Outside of the Graham orbit, she became the first Black woman to dance with the New York City Ballet. And she gained international fame as a teacher, using the pedagogical skills she'd developed at the University of Wisconsin. She could hold students spellbound just by walking across the studio floor—an exercise that sometimes took as long as forty-five minutes.

When you watch clips of Hinkson in action, ferociously executing a Graham-style contraction and release, you can understand why she bridled at limitations. She rejected racial categories and insisted that her art be recognized on its own terms. "We will have to speak of the 'Negro dancer,'" she once said, "until people are finally considered only on the grounds of their talent and merit."[1]

Let us, then, simply call Hinkson a dancer—one of the best of her time.

57

Alfred Lunt and Lynn Fontanne

Eyeball to Eyeball

The Ten Chimneys estate in Genesee Depot bulges with treasures from the long careers of husband-and-wife theater stars Alfred Lunt and Lynn Fontanne. On breaks from Broadway beginning in the 1920s, the couple filled their Waukesha County retreat with fanciful murals, Delft china, Spanish statues, rare books, and grandfather clocks from around the world. But on my tour of Ten Chimneys—now a National Historic Landmark open to the public—a simpler artifact caught my eye: Lunt and Fontanne's bed, barely wide enough for two bodies.

Amid such opulence, I wondered, why sleep with nary a millimeter between them?

By the end of the tour, it made perfect sense. Lunt and Fontanne had an intimacy for the ages. From the 1920s to the 1960s, they worked almost exclusively as a team, forging a naturalistic style of acting new to US theater. Critics remarked on their exceptional rapport in hits such as *The Guardsman* and *O Mistress Mine*, and colleagues admired their eyeball-to-eyeball preparation. "They would sit backstage on two chairs, facing each other with knees interlocked," said actor Gregory Peck. "Then they would go over and over their lines. When one did something the other thought was wrong, they'd bang their knees together, then start over again."[1]

After spending their days with knees interlocked in rehearsals, they spent their nights with bodies intertwined on that tiny bed. Following their deaths—Alfred in 1977, Lynn in 1983—they were buried side by side in Milwaukee's Forest Home Cemetery. And even when memories fade of their theatrical triumphs, Ten Chimneys will stand as a testament to their personal and professional communion.

Alfred grew up in Milwaukee and Waukesha and picnicked in Genesee Depot with his family. He pursued his lifelong love of acting at Waukesha's Carroll College before moving east for a career in the theater. And yet, the peaceful Genesee Depot landscape called to him. He bought property there in 1913, built a house, and continued to develop the estate after marrying English-born Fontanne in 1922. By the 1930s, it included a greenhouse; a log-cabin rehearsal studio imported from Sweden; a "Flirtation Room" reminiscent of a theatrical bedroom farce, with six doors leading every which way; and, yes, ten chimneys. The couple insisted on two clauses in their professional contract: one, that they always act together, and two, that they have summers off to restore body and soul in Genesee Depot.

As a result, the unincorporated hamlet became an unlikely power spot for the international arts community. Stars of stage and screen angled for a summertime invitation, and lucky visitors included Charlie Chaplin, Katharine Hepburn, Vivien Leigh, Montgomery Clift, and Carol Channing. Notable novelists, critics, and playwrights—like George S. Kaufman, Edna Ferber, W. Somerset Maugham, and Booth Tarkington—also lazed by the L-shaped pool. Theatrical superstars Helen Hayes, Laurence Olivier, and Noël Coward were among Lunt and Fontanne's closest friends, and the modern-day Ten Chimneys estate affixes their names to the bedrooms where they stayed. During her monthlong visits, Hayes even attended Sunday Mass at a nearby church.

"If you get to go to Ten Chimneys, you must have done something right," Carol Channing once said.[2] How lucky that now, we all get to go there.

58

Joan Cusack

Full-Tilt Screwball

Joan Cusack didn't just put in her time at the University of Wisconsin–Madison. She breathed in the countercultural air and developed an eccentric acting style that made her stand out in later movie and TV roles.

Cusack arrived at the UW in 1981 and joined Ark Improv, a group of actors who performed in pubs and a tiny studio space. Ark's sketches allowed her to loosen up, improvise, and find 1,001 offbeat ways to get a laugh. The troupe produced more than one idiosyncratic local star: Cusack and fellow Ark actor Chris Farley both went on to *Saturday Night Live*.

The quirky comic rhythms Cusack perfected at Ark served her well in *Broadcast News*, *Grosse Pointe Blank*, *Sixteen Candles*, *Say Anything . . .*, *High Fidelity*, the *Toy Story* franchise, *School of Rock*, and other admired films. Studios commonly cast her in second-banana roles: oddball girlfriends, principals, secretaries, sisters, housewives, and assistants. She received Oscar nominations for this type of performance in *Working Girl* and *In & Out*, and she won an Emmy Award for her turn as the phobic Sheila Jackson in *Shameless*.

But Cusack's shining moment came in one of the rare movies she dominates. Though *Addams Family Values* features comic scene-stealers Anjelica Huston, Raul Julia, and Christopher Lloyd, Cusack outdoes them all as a gold digger from hell: Marilyn Monroe from *Gentlemen Prefer Blondes* crossed with Cruella de Vil from *101 Dalmatians*. This is as close as Cusack comes onscreen to the full-tilt screwball acting she did in Madison.

Hired as the Addams family's nanny, Cusack's Debbie drops like a (blonde) bombshell into the topsy-turvy household. In this gothic netherworld, gloomy is good and beautiful is bad. Even among the flamboyantly wicked family members, however, Debbie stands out for her perversity. She sets her sights on Uncle Fester, who, while repulsive (*"Fester* means *rot*," he helpfully explains), is also rich. Cusack savors the demonic one-liners, playing against type as Fester's femme fatale.

The best word to describe her performance is *dreadful*. And in the Addams universe, that's the highest compliment.

59

Uta Hagen

"Perhaps I Was an Actress"

In 1937, seventeen-year-old Uta Hagen spent a dreary summer in her hometown of Madison. She had just finished her first semester at the University of Wisconsin and hated it. Why must she take math and biology classes when she cared only for theater? A few months earlier, she had traveled east to audition for Eva Le Gallienne's famous theater troupe. But landing a part with Le Gallienne seemed an impossible dream for a girl who had mostly acted in local school productions.

Or was it?

Miraculously, the call came, offering Hagen the role of Ophelia in *Hamlet*. "I climbed aboard a train to travel east with pounding heart and boundless expectation," she wrote in her autobiography, *Sources*.[1]

The teenager's "boundless expectation" was, in fact, fulfilled. With a gift for expressing the essence of her characters, Hagen emerged as one of the twentieth century's fiercest Broadway actors playing Desdemona in *Othello*, Blanche in *A Streetcar Named Desire*, and Martha in *Who's Afraid of Virginia Woolf?* Her equally fierce commitment to humanitarian values got her blacklisted during the 1950s Red Scare, which squelched her chance at achieving movie stardom. But not even McCarthyism could keep her from earning three Tony Awards, the National Medal of Arts, and a spot in the American Theater Hall of Fame. Some talent just can't be suppressed.

Hagen also worked as a theater teacher, and her books and classes inspired the likes of Jack Lemmon, Robert De Niro, and

Faye Dunaway. An apostle of psychological realism, she developed a method for helping actors draw on their own lived experience.

For Hagen, a good chunk of that experience occurred in Madison. She moved to town from Germany at age six when her father took a job as a UW art history professor. As an immigrant whose family preferred Bach to Badger football, she felt different from her neighbors on Adams Street—and often superior to them. But that didn't stop her from enjoying a quintessential Madison childhood.

In winter, she skated on frozen Lake Mendota; in spring, strolled on Picnic Point; in summer, vacationed at Rice Lake and Door County; and in fall, picked pumpkins on nearby farms. The rich sensory details in *Sources* leave no doubt that Wisconsin made an impression on her.

From a young age, Uta dabbled in role-playing and storytelling. She treated her Madison classmates to fantastical tales (a.k.a. lies) about being locked in closets back in Germany and fighting off deadly snakes at Devil's Lake. She graduated from playing elementary school elves and butterflies to more serious teenage parts that won praise in the *Wisconsin State Journal* and *Capital Times*. She also studied modern dance, experimented with theatrical makeup, and toured Wisconsin with her high school forensics team, reciting long speeches from George Bernard Shaw's *Saint Joan*. All the while, plays by Shakespeare, Chekhov, and Ibsen piled up on her desk and fired her imagination.

When Hagen turned fifteen, her older brother pulled strings to get her a part in a UW production of Noël Coward's *Hay Fever*. It proved a revelatory experience for both actor and audience. The breakout star gave herself permission to imagine a life on stage.

"It was a big step up the ladder from my high school plays," she wrote. "The stage itself was quite a contrast to the narrow platform in the high school auditorium where I'd played or to the gym that smelled of sweating feet. In Bascom Hall I started to believe, perhaps I was an actress."[2]

And indeed she was.

Champs

60

Jackie Robinson

True to Himself

Jackie Robinson stood up to death threats, physical assaults, and racial slurs when he integrated Major League Baseball in 1947. During the Jim Crow era, many white Americans deplored the idea of a Black man on the same field with white ballplayers. These included several of Robinson's own teammates, who signed a petition to keep him off the Brooklyn Dodgers. The shameful incident ranks among the low points of twentieth-century history—but a lesser-known Jackie Robinson story has a happier message about race relations. This one is set in Wisconsin.

Ronnie Rabinovitz was a white, eight-year-old Jewish boy from Sheboygan who admired the barrier-breaking Robinson. In 1954, his dad wrote the star a letter to ask if he might send a note to Ronnie—a longshot request that, incredibly, Robinson granted. Two months later, father and son attended a game between the Dodgers and the Milwaukee Braves at County Stadium to see their hero up close. When Robinson emerged from the clubhouse, Ronnie called out, "Hey, Jackie, I'm Ronnie Rabinovitz, remember me?" To his amazement, Robinson answered, "Yes, your dad is the one who wrote me a letter, and I wrote you back. Stay in touch!"[1]

And that's just what Ronnie did. The two continued to exchange greetings at Dodgers games in Milwaukee and began a longtime correspondence. Jackie supported Ronnie in his physical fitness efforts and congratulated him on his bar mitzvah. He also shared his perspective on life, writing, "I learned a long time ago that a person must be true to himself if he is to succeed. He must be willing to stand by his principles even at the possible loss of prestige."[2]

Jackie Robinson, pictured in Milwaukee in 1954, hoped to make the next generation more tolerant than his own. WHI IMAGE ID 65670

That sums up Robinson's conduct on the ballfield. His belief in the American promise of equal rights allowed him to face his trials with courage and dignity. But why would he go to the trouble of explaining all this to a child—a white child from faraway Sheboygan, no less?

We can only guess. My theory is that Robinson saw in Ronnie Rabinovitz a soul yet to be corrupted by prejudice. Here was a chance to influence the next generation, one that might prove more tolerant than his own.

If that's what Robinson meant to do, the strategy worked. After his idol died in 1972, Rabinovitz sent a letter to Rachel Robinson, Jackie's widow. He explained what Jackie had taught him over the course of their unlikely friendship: that all people deserve respect, regardless of background or skin color.

Come to think of it, that's just what he taught me, a white child from St. Louis, when I learned about him in the 1960s. And so it goes for children who learn about him to this day. Jackie Robinson continues to shape the minds of impressionable youth—and who better?

61

Bart Starr

To the Gates of Hell

Bart Starr once said that for a quarterback to be successful, "his teammates must be willing to go to the gates of hell with him."[1] And that's exactly where Starr led the Green Bay Packers in 1967's National Football League championship game against the Dallas Cowboys—a subzero pit of suffering now known as the Ice Bowl.

At one time, few would have thought Starr capable of such leadership. His father, a stern US Air Force sergeant, didn't consider him tough enough to succeed in football. But Bart worked on being more aggressive, excelled on his high school team in Montgomery, Alabama, and emerged as a top prospect among college recruiters. Still, he chose the University of Alabama, not because it had the best program but because that was where his high school sweetheart, Cherry Louise Morton, planned to enroll. Not exactly a move that said "future Hall of Famer."

Starr had mixed success as a college quarterback, and he joined the Packers as the lowly two-hundredth overall pick in the 1956 NFL draft. He continued his self-improvement program, throwing thousands of passes through a tire hanging from a tree in advance of his rookie season. But that didn't pay off in Green Bay, where he notched a dismal 3–15–1 record in his first three years. When new coach Vince Lombardi arrived in 1959, he thought Starr might be "too polite and maybe just a little too self-effacing to be the real bold, tough quarterback that a quarterback must be in the National Football League."[2]

On closer inspection, however, Lombardi recognized the young player's strong arm, good ball-handling instincts, and intelligence.

What he lacked was confidence—and that's where Lombardi's brilliant offensive system came into play. Starr studied it, mastered it, and led the Packers to league championships in 1961, 1962, and 1965. The next year, he won the NFL's Most Valuable Player Award while steamrolling the Kansas City Chiefs in the first Super Bowl. Control freak though he was, Lombardi came to trust Starr's play-calling ability in the huddle.

While other Packers fled Wisconsin in the offseason, Starr settled into Green Bay with Cherry—yes, he'd married his high school sweetheart—and involved himself in the community. The couple founded the Rawhide Boys Ranch in New London to help Wisconsin's at-risk youth. "Playing quarterback in Green Bay is about more than winning championships," Starr said, a message sometimes lost on his successors Brett Favre and Aaron Rodgers.[3] To him, playing in Green Bay was also about class and compassion.

Oh, and courage—a quality he would need for surviving the diabolical Ice Bowl. With the wind chill at thirty-six below and the heating system on the fritz, Lambeau Field transformed into an ice rink. Players developed frostbite, and one fan died of exposure. Starr faced a 17–14 deficit as he began a seventy-yard drive near the end of the fourth quarter, throwing passes with frozen fingers. Within inches of the goal line, and with sixteen seconds on the clock, he made a momentous decision with Lombardi's blessing: an attempt to sneak in the ball himself rather than risk a handoff on the slippery turf.

Starr had led his teammates to the gates of hell and would take full responsibility for their fate. In fact, he decided not to tell others in the huddle what he had planned. After the snap, and an epic block by Jerry Kramer, the determined quarterback dove into the end zone—and into history. The Packers' last-minute win endures as an all-time highlight of professional sports.

As Starr took the field for that final drive, Green Bay linebacker Ray Nitschke had shouted, "Don't let me down!"[4] Needless to say, letdowns weren't part of the Bart Starr playbook.

62

Mark Johnson

The Miracle on Ice

The US men's hockey team was an unlikely gold medalist at the 1980 Olympics. And Madison's Mark Johnson was its unlikely MVP.

The team consisted of inexperienced college recruits who'd played together for just six months. The Soviets, by contrast, were a long-running professional operation considered unbeatable. They had won gold in the previous four Olympics and recently crushed a team of National Hockey League all-stars 6–0. On top of that, they'd overwhelmed the extraordinarily young US Olympic team in an exhibition game just before the 1980 winter games began in Lake Placid, New York. "They could have won by fifteen if they wanted to," Johnson admitted after the game. "It was almost like they were giving us a lesson out there."[1] Chances for US success in the Olympics: next to zero.

The United States was undergoing a "crisis of confidence," as President Jimmy Carter had put it a few months earlier. The country struggled with high gas prices, unemployment, inflation, and a hostage situation in Iran. Meanwhile, the Soviets flexed their muscle by invading Afghanistan in late 1979. Most Americans took it for granted that their upcoming confrontation with the Soviet hockey machine would be yet another Cold War humiliation.

Was twenty-two-year-old Mark Johnson the man to flip that script? No sane person would have bet on it. At a mere 5'9" and 150 pounds, the center from UW–Madison did not look the part of a giant slayer. He was also humble and mild-mannered, laudable qualities in anyone but a superstar athlete.

On the other hand, Johnson had spent his whole life training for this moment, starting with pickup games on frozen Madison ponds. His father, Bob, was the renowned men's hockey coach for University of Wisconsin–Madison and an admirer of the Soviet team. Bob ran drills where Mark and his teammates impersonated various Soviet players, right down to the names sewn onto their jerseys. So even as a teenager, Mark was getting inside the heads of his future Olympic opponents.

Despite his small stature, Johnson distinguished himself on the UW team with hard work, smarts, and skill, winning the conference's Rookie of the Year award in 1977. But facing the Soviets would be altogether different from playing the University of Minnesota. After forming the US Olympic team in 1979, Coach Herb Brooks ran the young players ragged with wind sprints— sometimes in the dark, after custodians had shut off the practice facility's lights. It helped them reach a level of physical fitness that would have put Superman to shame.

In the medal-round match with the Soviets on February 22, 1980, no one was surprised to see the US down 2–1 near the end of the first period. With one second left, players began skating off the ice, but Johnson turned the intensity up rather than down. He grabbed a rebound, expertly wove between two defenders, and, holding onto the puck an instant longer than the Soviet goalie expected him to, scored one of the most famous goals in hockey history. Going into the second period tied was just the morale boost his team needed.

By the third period they were down 3–2, but Johnson again tied the score, extracting the puck from a defender's skates and smashing it between the goalie's legs. This was the moment when the team—as well as people glued to their TVs—began to think the unthinkable. Could the United States *win* this game? After a go-ahead goal by Mike Eruzione and ten minutes of tireless defense (thank you, wind sprints), they did, prompting broadcaster Al Michaels's famous exclamation: "Do you believe in miracles?!"

The game would forever be known as the Miracle on Ice, picked by *Sports Illustrated* as the greatest sports moment of the twentieth

As a member of the 1978 UW–Madison men's hockey team, Mark Johnson
did not seem like a player who would go on to beat the unbeatable Soviets.
UNIVERSITY OF WISCONSIN-MADISON ARCHIVES

century. Wild celebrations broke out from coast to coast, and President Carter put in a congratulatory call to Brooks. For the time being, it seemed, the national crisis of confidence had ended.

The Americans went on to beat Finland for the gold medal, fueled by two more goals from Johnson. He earned most valuable player honors with a team-leading eleven points, along with the nickname "Magic." Eruzione called him "the best player and most important player on our team. We don't win without Mark. . . . When we needed big goals, Mark scored them."[2]

Just one person refused to call Mark Johnson the team's most important player: Mark Johnson himself. Over the next few decades, as an NHL standout and then the championship-winning coach of the UW women's hockey program, he downplayed his own role while praising a world-class example of teamwork. And he never lorded his legendary stature over anybody, including his UW players. "[Johnson] doesn't talk to us about that [Olympic] team," one of them said. "It's always about us and our team and not his past. He's just a nice, friendly, humble guy."[3]

In retrospect, humility doesn't seem like such a bad quality for a superstar athlete after all.

63

Hank Aaron

Rookie of the Year

Hank Aaron spent most of his career in Milwaukee with the Braves and Brewers, setting career records for home runs and runs batted in and earning his own room in the National Baseball Hall of Fame. But Hammerin' Hank has a lesser-known association with another Wisconsin city. After signing him in 1952, the Braves sent the eighteen-year-old to the Eau Claire Bears, their Class C farm team in the Northern League. Aaron later acknowledged that he felt unprepared for this overwhelmingly white community, having grown up in segregated Mobile, Alabama.

Many Eau Claire residents felt just as unprepared for Aaron when he arrived in June. Some gawked at the Black ballplayer as if he'd just beamed down from outer space. One waitress at a downtown restaurant refused to serve him.

But a heartening thing happened in the summer of 1952. As the shy kid tore up the Northern League on his way to a Rookie of the Year award, folks in Eau Claire began to get along with him. White families extended dinner invitations, and Aaron accepted. He became particularly close to one family and embarked on a romance with their teenage daughter. The two often sat on the front porch holding hands—a daring gesture in that racist era—and caused no public outcry. As Aaron said later, "I was treated as fair as could be in Eau Claire."[1]

Compare this to the treatment he received on his next minor league posting in Jacksonville, Florida, where white fans shouted slurs and mailed him death threats. The team forbade its three Black players from using the same locker rooms as their white teammates, so Aaron had to suit up at a segregated hotel. He persevered in the face of such cruelty with the same dignity he showed throughout his Major League career.

During the civil rights struggles of the 1960s and beyond, Aaron and Eau Claire continued to model racial harmony. He returned to the city several times, notably in 1994, when thousands attended the dedication of a statue commemorating his memorable season with the Bears. "A lot of things happened to me in my twenty-three years as a ballplayer," he said of the event, "but nothing touched me more than that day in Eau Claire."[2]

Given the long, sad history of US race relations, who *wouldn't* be touched by this vision of mutual love and respect?

64

Eric and Beth Heiden

Good as Gold

In the mid-1970s, Madisonians encountered a strange sight in a local park: two teenagers furiously duck-walking around a two-hundred-yard dirt track. Eric Heiden, just over six feet, and his younger sister Beth Heiden, just over five feet, appeared to be speed-skating, but on dry land.

The muscle-building duck walk formed part of the training regimen that soon turned the siblings into international sensations. They appeared together on the cover of *Time* magazine in February 1980, looking much as they did in that Madison park but this time on real ice: crouching, arms swinging, skates flashing, eyes burning with conviction. The headline dubbed them "Good as Gold," predicting spectacular success in the Winter Olympics.

Twenty-one-year-old Eric and twenty-year-old Beth earned the hype through sheer force of will. As kids, they skated relentlessly on Madison's frozen Lake Mendota. They rigged up a homemade gym in their west-side house, including a sheet of plastic in the basement where they could simulate a skating motion in their stocking feet. Eric developed tree-trunk thighs twenty-seven inches in circumference, forcing him to buy pants several sizes too large for his waist. Beth lacked a typical speedskater's physique, being significantly shorter and lighter than her competitors, but she compensated with pure ferocity. Eric called her "a sparrow with a tiger hidden inside her."[1]

The siblings made a daily seventy-five-mile drive to an Olympic skating rink in West Allis, rushing through their high school homework along the way. And they began a series of triumphs. After failing to medal at the 1976 Olympics at age seventeen, Eric stunned the speedskating world by winning the World Championships in 1977—the first American man to hold that title since 1891. He did it again in 1978 and 1979, setting a mere six world records during those two years. Meanwhile, Beth won the women's speedskating World Junior Championships in 1978 and 1979, plus the World Championships in 1979—the first American woman to do so since 1936. By this time, the siblings were both students at the University of Wisconsin–Madison and poised to conquer the globe at the 1980 Winter Olympics in Lake Placid, New York.

Beth suffered an ankle injury but still won a bronze medal in the 3,000-meter race. Eric, meanwhile, turned in one of the finest performances in sports history. In five races, he set five Olympic records and one world mark, becoming the first person to win five individual golds at a single Olympics. What's more, he accomplished this feat in distances ranging from a sprint to a marathon. Stunned observers struggled for comparisons, ranking his achievement with Joe DiMaggio's fifty-six-game hitting streak in 1941 and Wilt Chamberlain's one-hundred-point game in 1962. It would become an inspiration to generations of Wisconsin's champion skaters, including Dan Jansen and Christine Witty, who were born in West Allis; Verona's Casey Fitzrandolph; Kewaskum's Jordan Stolz; and Bonnie Blair, who now lives in Delafield.

At this point, Eric's rivals likely abandoned all hope of beating him. The coach of the Norwegian speedskating team admitted, "We just hope he retires."[2]

And that's just what he did soon after the Olympics, along with Beth. They had no interest in milking their speedskating success. Both made a point of downplaying their heroic stature, fending off endorsement deals and even pooh-poohing the very idea of Olympic honors. "The medals don't mean that much," Eric insisted. "The effort I put into the races is what's important. The medals will probably sit where all the rest are, in my mom's dresser, gathering dust."[3]

What did interest the siblings was facing down the next challenge. Both turned to cycling, and both won major races. Beth became a championship cross-country skier and Eric a respected orthopedic surgeon. Given their discipline and determination, these two would obviously succeed at anything they set their minds to, with one exception.

"I don't want people following me around, putting me on a pedestal," Eric cautioned after his Olympic triumph.[4] But that's the rare goal he failed to achieve. In 1999, the Associated Press chose him as the Winter Olympian of the Century.

65

The Racine Belles and Kenosha Comets

All-American Legends

A major event in sports history took place in September 1943. Two teams played in the inaugural championship series of the All-American Girls Professional Baseball League, the forerunner of women's professional league sports. Both were from Wisconsin, and both grabbed the public imagination.

Chicago Cubs owner Philip K. Wrigley founded the league in 1943 to keep fans coming to ballparks while male players served in World War II. He held tryouts for women around the United States and Canada and picked the top prospects for the first four teams: the Racine Belles, Kenosha Comets, Rockford Peaches, and South Bend Blue Sox. The athletes had the rare opportunity to get decent salaries, play for big crowds, and bask in media attention. Unfortunately, they couldn't avoid the era's sexist attitudes.

Unlike their hard-living male counterparts in Major League Baseball, the women had to follow strict guidelines for grooming and manners. The patriarchs who ran their league required them to wear makeup, abstain from drinking, and don "ladylike" uniforms. (Try sliding into third while wearing a short skirt.) They had to obey chaperones and even attend Helena Rubinstein's charm school to learn the approved ways of walking in high heels. "Always appear in feminine attire when not actively engaged in practice or playing ball," warned the league's rules of conduct. "Boyish bobs are not permissible and in general your hair should be well groomed at all times with longer hair preferable to short haircuts."[1]

When the league debuted, the press and the public initially viewed the players as novelties. But as with Rosie the Riveter types who were participating in wartime industries, they quickly showed their stuff. "Maybe at first the men came out to see the legs," recalled Pepper Paire Davis, a catcher and infielder for the Racine Belles. "But they stuck around when they realized they were seeing a darn good brand of baseball."[2]

The league proved popular in Wisconsin, and the state's teams excelled. Kenosha's Helen Nicol emerged as the 1943 season's best pitcher, with 31 wins, 220 strikeouts, and a 1.81 earned run average. Racine's Eleanor Dapkus reigned as the season's top slugger with ten home runs. In the all-Wisconsin championship series, the Belles bested the Comets in three straight games, with Racine catcher Irene Hickson batting a torrid .417. The league's impressive attendance for 1943—176,000—meant it was there to stay.

For a while, anyway. The league expanded to ten teams, and attendance rose to nearly a million in 1948. But recruiting new players proved difficult, and cash-strapped franchises cut back on expenses. Plus, as Rosie the Riveter gave way to June Cleaver, 1950s norms urged women toward home rather than home plate. In 1954, the league shut down amid a backlash against women playing baseball. Hickson went to work in a Racine department store, and Nicol was hired at Kenosha's American Motors.

Still, the players had paved the way for the Women's National Basketball Association, Women's Tennis Association, and other professional women's sports organizations. They were ultimately recognized with a permanent display in the National Baseball Hall of Fame in 1988 and immortalized in the 1992 movie *A League of Their Own.*

The attention came as a shock to many of the trailblazers who thought the country had forgotten about them. Joyce Barnes McCoy, who pitched for the Kenosha Comets in 1943, was astonished by the warm reception at a ballgame in her native Hutchinson, Kansas, a half-century after her playing career had ended.

"They asked me to come and throw out a pitch," she said. "I never experienced anything like that. Some of the officials of Hutchinson were there, so they introduced us. And when they introduced me, I stood up, and that whole grandstand was alive with yelling and hollering. I took off my hat and waved at them, and they started in again. And all the umpires took their hats off, and I had to autograph everything."[3]

Yes, hats off to Joyce Barnes McCoy and the other Wisconsin players from the All-American Girls Professional Baseball League. It's good to know that, by the end of their lives, people saw them for what they really were: all-American legends.

66

Kareem Abdul-Jabbar

The Luck of the Bucks

One of the most momentous coin flips in sports history went Wisconsin's way. In 1969, the Milwaukee Bucks held the worst record in the National Basketball Association's eastern division. That positioned them for a showdown with the western division's woeful Phoenix Suns over who would get the number-one college draft pick. The prize: Kareem Abdul-Jabbar (then known as Lew Alcindor), the astonishing 7'2" center who'd led UCLA to three consecutive national titles.

Neither team wanted to leave the coin flip to . . . well, chance. The Suns polled their fans about whether to pick heads or tails. Bucks general manager John Erickson consulted with Las Vegas oddsmakers, who suggested letting the opponent make the call. That's how Suns general manager Jerry Colangelo ended up with the 1964 Kennedy half-dollar between his thumb and forefinger, calling heads. He flipped the coin, caught it, and—to his eternal regret—flipped it one more time onto the back of his hand. Tails brought Abdul-Jabbar to Milwaukee to launch arguably the greatest career in NBA history.

In his first season, Kareem averaged nearly twenty-nine points and fifteen rebounds a game and was named Rookie of the Year. In his second, he led the once-dismal Bucks—in just their third year as an expansion team—to an NBA championship while earning the Most Valuable Player Award. Afterward, he announced his conversion to Islam and his new name.

Abdul-Jabbar starred in Milwaukee for the next four seasons, scoring at will with his lethal sky hook and picking up two more

Basketball phenom Kareem Abdul-Jabbar (second from left) signed with the Los Angeles Lakers in 1975 after an extraordinary run with the Milwaukee Bucks. UCLA LIBRARY SPECIAL COLLECTIONS

MVP Awards. He also displayed a commitment to civil rights that set the stage for generations of activist athletes, including quarterback and Fond du Lac native Colin Kaepernick. In 1974, however, he requested a trade to a team on the East or West Coast, for personal reasons. "I don't have any family or friends here," he told the *Los Angeles Times*. "The things I relate to don't happen to be in this city to any meaningful degree. Culturally, what I'm about and what Milwaukee is about are two different things. The reason I haven't commented on this before is I don't want to take a knock at Milwaukee or the people here and have them think they're unworthy of me. That's not what it's all about."[1]

Even if it wasn't, Milwaukee fans despaired when Abdul-Jabbar headed to the Los Angeles Lakers, where he won three more MVP Awards and five more NBA championships. But in 2021, Kareem made amends by returning to Milwaukee to cheer on the Bucks as they competed for their second NBA championship against— who else?—the Phoenix Suns. He had kind words for the city, particularly its tolerance for his religious convictions. "The Milwaukee fans were always very supportive of me, even when I converted to Islam and changed my name," he said. "That had to be a hard transition for them, especially fifty years ago."[2]

During the 2021 finals, Abdul-Jabbar posted a video that harked back to the fateful coin toss of 1969. "Some fifty odd years ago, the Bucks and Suns had to flip a coin to see who would get the opportunity to draft me," he said, wearing his number thirty-three Milwaukee jersey and a playful smile. "This time, *I'm* taking charge of it."

He flipped a coin and predicted, "Bucks in six!"[3] And that's exactly what happened.

67

Kit Saunders-Nordeen

The Fight for Title IX

As a child in the 1970s, I believed feminism was the future. On television, "liberated women" got the better of men on the sitcoms *Bewitched* and *Maude*. On Top 40 radio, Helen Reddy proclaimed "I Am Woman." My family closely followed 1973's "Battle of the Sexes," in which women's tennis star Billie Jean King walloped the self-proclaimed male chauvinist pig Bobby Riggs. My own mother fought for women's right to use the so-called men's racquetball courts at her gym. Even Virginia Slims cigarette commercials praised women for coming "a long way, baby, to get where you've got to today."

In elementary school, I failed to perceive the condescension in that ad. Nor did I understand that the real-life patriarchy would not roll over as easily as Samantha Stephens's dimwitted husband on *Bewitched*. Second-wave feminists had a fight on their hands—one no less daunting than the battles Susan B. Anthony, Sojourner Truth, and Alice Paul had waged for suffrage in the nineteenth and early twentieth centuries.

Consider Title IX of the Education Amendments of 1972, which prohibited sex-based discrimination in education and programs receiving federal funds. The new regulation meant, among other things, that women deserved and were ostensibly guaranteed equal opportunity in college athletics. Problem solved, right?

Suffice it to say that equality didn't materialize with a flick of the president's pen. By and large, the men in charge of college athletics programs still weren't inclined to play fair. Like the officials who barred my mother from the racquetball courts, they dragged their feet and made excuses when it came to enforcing the new law.

The conflict played out on campuses all over the country, including the University of Wisconsin–Madison. For years, Kit Saunders-Nordeen had struggled in her role as women's coordinator for the UW club sports program, whose administrators often treated female athletes as second-class citizens. Unlike their male peers, the women playing club sports had to pay their own expenses for overnight trips. They also received limited access to practice facilities, and a dearth of uniforms forced underpaid women coaches into doing their teams' laundry.

When Title IX passed, Saunders-Nordeen saw a ray of hope. The good news was that Chancellor Edwin Young appointed a committee to improve the status of women's athletics. The bad news was that the committee included no women athletes. Even worse, Athletic Director Elroy Hirsch, who chaired the committee, showed little interest in calling meetings. One enraged member, Muriel Sloan of the women's physical education department, berated Hirsch for his "nonfunctioning committee." Neurophysiology professor Ruth Bleier followed up with her own scorching letter to Hirsch in 1973:

> We demand immediate and equal use of all facilities: tracks, fields, courts and pools, locker rooms, and showers. . . . We demand adequate and equal (as needed) funding for all women's sports teams, including salaries for coaches with full-time academic appointments and expenses for training and competition. Anything less than this must be negotiated with us and other women in athletics and justified to our satisfaction. We do not want to hear again about inadequacy of facilities, space, and time. If they are inadequate, we will share equally with men in the inadequacy. The burden is no longer ours to wait. We have waited too long. The moral and, now, the legal burden is yours.[1]

In 1973, a complaint was filed against the university with the US Office of Civil Rights. According to Doug Moe's 2022 biography of Saunders-Nordeen, *The Right Thing to Do*, Chancellor Young now understood that the women meant business. He replaced Hirsch as committee chair, and the bureaucratic wheels started turning. It took another year—and a panel discussion during which attendees hissed and booed Hirsch's every utterance—for the UW to create the women's intercollegiate athletic program, with Saunders-Nordeen as director. In the following decades, the UW women's teams won national championships in rowing, hockey, volleyball, basketball, and cross country while producing Olympic gold medalists Carie Graves in rowing, Carly Piper in swimming, and Rose Lavelle in soccer.

"Freedom is never voluntarily given by the oppressor," observed Martin Luther King Jr. in 1963. "It must be demanded by the oppressed."[2] At UW–Madison, the oppressed women made their demands and refused to give up until they won their rights.

RIP male chauvinist pigs.

68

George Poage

Leaping the Hurdles

I spent my childhood borrowing library books about pioneering Black athletes: Jackie Robinson, Althea Gibson, Jack Johnson. Oddly, I never ran across the name George Poage, the first Black American to win an Olympic medal. Therein lies a tale—one of triumph and tragedy.

Poage had risen from humble circumstances to distinguish himself as an athlete, scholar, and singer during the Jim Crow era. But racism and homophobia made it impossible for him to parlay these talents into a career. He fell into obscurity and spent the last decades of his life as a postal clerk. Even his hometown of La Crosse seemed to have forgotten about him. A century later, the city still had no statue commemorating his historic feat.

Poage's parents, who had survived enslavement, moved the family from Hannibal, Missouri, to La Crosse in 1884 in search of a better life. His mother, a maid, harbored big dreams for George. As the only Black student in his 1899 graduating class at La Crosse High School, he delivered a commencement address on "the race problem," declaring that many Black people were "too severely censured and unjustly dealt with."[1] Just three years earlier, the US Supreme Court had shamefully affirmed segregation's constitutionality in *Plessy v. Ferguson*.

Poage excelled at La Crosse High as both a student and a runner. He first gained notice when bystanders saw him sprinting through Burns Park across from the school. On the track team, he set a state record for the fifty-yard dash. His athletic prowess, combined with an enthusiastic recommendation from the high school principal, earned him admission to the overwhelmingly white University of Wisconsin in 1899.

On the Madison campus, Poage sang in a choir, debated, studied history and political science, and joined the track team as its first Black member. Sportswriters described him with condescending epithets that marked him as an outsider.

Poage won Big Ten championships in the 440-yard dash and 220-yard hurdles. His fame spread throughout the state, and the Milwaukee Athletic Club recruited him to compete in the 1904 Olympics in St. Louis. Despite the demeaning treatment of Black athletes—including segregated and inferior housing—Poage captured bronze medals in the 400- and 200-meter hurdles.

But at the height of his success, he found himself with limited options in an increasingly bigoted nation. Moving from Missouri to Minnesota to Illinois, Poage cycled through jobs as a high school teacher, principal, farmer, cook, and restaurateur. In 1924, he settled into a secure position in a Chicago post office. The anonymity likely appealed to him as a Black man who may have been gay, according to some historians. He knew he could be brutalized, jailed, or even killed for simply existing.

Poage died in 1962, missing out on the Civil Rights Act of 1964, the Voting Rights Act of 1965, and the 1969 Stonewall Uprising. He also missed out on seeing that statue in his honor, finally erected by the city of La Crosse in 2016. Its four figures show Poage in various stages of a race, from crouching to sprinting to clearing a hurdle to raising his arms in victory. For a man who won two Olympic medals against all odds, the medium—bronze—is poetically apt.

69

Gwen Jorgensen

The World's Speediest Accountant

Gwen Jorgensen expected to spend her life as an accountant, toiling eighty hours a week in the Milwaukee office of Ernst & Young. Instead, she became an Olympic gold medalist—and then did something even more surprising.

Jorgensen grew up in Waukesha as a quiet rule-follower. For an introvert, the pool promised solitude, so she entered swim contests starting at age eight. Meanwhile, she astonished her elementary school with a now-legendary run around the track. She was supposed to do a four-lap mile—and did—but returned so soon that teachers thought she'd completed only three laps. They made her go back and run another one.

Jorgensen concentrated on swimming at the University of Wisconsin–Madison in 2004, but she fell short of her Olympic dream. Indeed, she didn't even qualify for the NCAA meets that would have made the Olympics a possibility. When a UW coach approached her about running track instead of swimming, she assumed she'd be out of her league.

She wasn't, to say the least. By the end of her college career, Jorgensen won Big Ten championships in the 3,000 and 5,000 meters and finally made those important NCAA meets. Nevertheless, she set aside her Olympic ambitions for a more sensible post-college career, putting her master's degree in accounting to use at Ernst & Young. During her few hours away from taxes each week, she jogged as a hobby.

Jorgensen's life took another unexpected turn when a representative from USA Triathlon approached her about training for the

Gwen Jorgensen set aside her spreadsheets at a
Milwaukee accounting firm to win the 2011
Triathlon World Cup. MARTIN PUTZ, CC-BY-SA-3.0

team. She had never competed in triathlon, an endurance sport
that includes swimming, cycling, and running. In fact, she didn't
even own a bicycle and had no experience with a road bike. Gwen
was reluctant, but in 2010 she consented to train while staying at
Ernst & Young. That meant rising at three thirty in the morning to
swim, bike, and run most days before work.

Just two years later, Jorgensen qualified for the 2012 Olympics
and finally put aside her spreadsheets. She yearned for a medal but
suffered a flat tire during her cycling segment. As she crossed the
finish line in thirty-eighth place, a single thought went through her
head: Olympic gold in 2016.

When Jorgensen sets her mind to something, watch out. She worked with superhuman focus, willing herself to be a champion. After an unprecedented string of wins in World Triathlon Series races, she competed in Rio in 2016 and won the United States' first Olympic gold medal in triathlon. And for the first time at a finish line, she cried.

But then came another twist in this unpredictable life. A year after her Rio triumph, Jorgensen shocked the international triathlon community by announcing her pregnancy and her retirement. She wasn't leaving athletics—she was just switching to the marathon. Her goal: Olympic gold in 2020.

Seven weeks after giving birth, Jorgensen began training with characteristic intensity. Within six months, she won the 10,000 meters at the Stanford Invitational, but an injury knocked her out of competition for the Olympics. That necessitated another change of course: a switch to shorter distances, with an eye on the 2024 games. Which, at age thirty-eight, she didn't make.

At this point, I don't care if Jorgensen never wins another race. She's already made a statement with her flexible approach to life's journey. At each crossroads, she has considered new opportunities with appropriate skepticism but also an open mind. Then, after deciding to pursue an unfamiliar challenge, she goes all in.

"We should all set big goals and then go after them," Jorgensen said in 2018, a motto that would sound trite if she hadn't definitively proved it true.[1]

70

Fred Merkle

One Lapse in Judgment

I loved baseball as a kid, but I lived in fear of making a mistake on the field. As a junior baseball-history scholar, I'd read way too much about Fred Merkle, the Wisconsin native who paid a steep price for committing the game's most infamous baserunning error.

Born in Watertown, Merkle joined the New York Giants in 1907 as a teenage infielder. His career looked promising until a wild game against the Chicago Cubs in New York on September 23, 1908. The teams were tied for first place in the final game of the season, playing each other for the pennant. The score stood at 1–1 in the bottom of the ninth inning, with Merkle on first base and another runner on third. The next batter singled, the runner on third scored, and the Giants appeared to have won the game.

Fans poured out of the stands. To avoid the pandemonium, Merkle dashed for the dugout without getting all the way to second base—his fatal mistake. A Cubs player noticed he hadn't tagged the base and managed to get hold of a ball (possibly not even the game ball) amid the chaos. He touched second, meaning that Merkle was technically out and the game was still tied.

With thousands of fans screaming on the field, play could not resume that day. Tragically for Merkle, the Cubs won the makeup game and thus the pennant.

Merkle's mistake earned him the nickname "Bonehead," and it trailed him for the rest of his life. Despite an admirable baseball career that included six World Series, he remained a laughingstock for that one lapse in judgment. The word *Merkle* even entered baseball slang, meaning a profoundly stupid play. When he died in 1956, the *New York Times* headline inevitably referenced the error.

That might have been the end of the story, but Merkle's hometown came to his rescue. Watertown residents looked at the whole of Merkle's life, not just the one lapse. They discovered a modest, decent man who stood up to adversity. Rather than quitting in shame, he stuck with baseball and distinguished himself as a champion. Rather than lashing out at those who called him "Bonehead," he bore the insults with grace.

In 2005, Watertown erected a monument to Merkle: a black stone marker picturing his determined face and noting his outstanding talent and intelligence. The city also named a field after him in Washington Park.

I hope the kids playing baseball on Fred Merkle Field draw a lesson from their local hero. I know I have. He showed that our worth isn't defined by errors but by our ability to transcend them.

Boundary Breakers

71

Jim Lovell

"Houston, We've Had a Problem"

As a child, I loved superheroes and astronauts—and to me, those two American archetypes seemed equally fantastical. Superman could fly beyond Earth's atmosphere; so could astronauts. Wonder Woman performed death-defying feats without flinching; so did astronauts. When I finally learned the difference—superheroes are made up and astronauts are real—I traded in my comic books for biographies of Jim Lovell. I wanted to be a real-life hero like him.

It would have been enough if Lovell had just set a record for the longest time in space during 1965's Gemini 7 mission. But he also became the first person to orbit the moon during 1968's Apollo 8 mission. And to cap off his career, this guardian of the galaxy improvised one of the most daring recoveries in the annals of aviation during 1970's Apollo 13 disaster.

The mission was fifty-five hours into its journey to the moon when Commander Lovell radioed Mission Control with an incongruously low-key alarm: "Houston, we've had a problem."[1] A tank had exploded, causing a sudden drop in oxygen and power. Almost 200,000 miles from Earth, Lovell and his crewmates, Fred Haise and Jack Swigert, calmly got to work repurposing the lunar module as a sort of lifeboat.

Later in life, when I had a chance to interview Lovell, you can guess the first thing I asked: "How does a normal person turn into a real-life superhero?" It was more than a journalistic inquiry. I still had faint hopes of becoming heroic myself, and I wanted information.

Jim Lovell developed his superhuman self-confidence
as an only child in Milwaukee. NASA IMAGE ID S69-62241

I forgot that an essential part of Lovell's valor involved humility.
Of course he didn't want to address the subject of his own greatness,
preferring to explain the nuts and bolts of the Apollo 13 rescue. He
also enjoyed talking about his flight-obsessed childhood in Milwaukee, where he invented his own "powder rocket" from an old mailing
tube. Since his family had little money, college seemed out of reach,
but he discovered a scholarship program that sent him to the University of Wisconsin and then the US Naval Academy to fulfill his dream
of becoming a pilot. He showed a knack for flying experimental air-
craft and completing dangerous missions with a shrug.

NASA saw a star in the making, accepting Lovell as an astronaut
in 1962. In 1968, while orbiting the moon, he was awestruck by the
sight of his own planet from such a distance. "Earth got very small,

and I could put my thumb up and hide it completely," he told me. "It gave me the thought that that was my home back there, and I hope I get back. Because it was really just a small dot in space."[2] Clearly, the superhero was human after all.

At the end of our talk, I tried a different version of my first question: How did an ordinary Wisconsin kid develop "the right stuff," in Tom Wolfe's memorable phrase? This time, Lovell hesitated, thought about it for a second, then—in what seemed to me a *Citizen Kane*–style "Rosebud" moment—turned back to his experience as an only child in Milwaukee.

"Well, my father died when I was young, so my mother raised me," he said, departing from his comfortable talking points. "That was quite a time, because she worked, and I was alone. I think that gave me a lot of self-confidence to take care of myself."[3]

Lovell finished his reverie with the understatement of the century: "And I think that was well worthwhile."

72

Jeffrey Erlanger

It's You I Like, Mister Rogers

Jeffrey Erlanger began his journey through the Madison medical system as a baby in the 1970s, requiring spinal surgery that left him without the use of his limbs. He got an electric wheelchair at age four, and a year later, he needed another dangerous procedure. To soften the blow, his parents offered to grant him a wish, but they didn't anticipate his seemingly impossible request: to meet Pittsburgh-based Fred Rogers, the gentle host of the children's television program *Mister Rogers' Neighborhood*. Like so many kids around the country, Jeffrey liked to imagine himself a resident of Rogers's fictional neighborhood, where he'd feel loved and valued regardless of his differences.

The Erlangers left it to Jeffrey's older sister, Lisa, to write a letter. Rather than getting lost in the mountain of fan mail, her heartfelt note found its way to Rogers, who offered to meet the family for breakfast at the Pfister Hotel during a 1975 trip to Milwaukee. There, they discovered that the star's nurturing TV persona did not switch off with the studio lights. He and Jeffrey bonded over the meal. A snapshot exists of Fred helping cut the boy's food.

Miraculously, Jeffrey survived his surgery. He stayed in touch with his special friend, and in 1981, he maneuvered his wheelchair onto the set for a segment of *Mister Rogers' Neighborhood*. With no script and no rehearsal, the two merely chatted with the cameras rolling. "This is my friend Jeff Erlanger," says Rogers, sitting on a porch step in his signature cardigan sweater. "He's one of my neighbors here, and I asked him if he would come by today because I wanted you to meet him, and I wanted you to see his electric wheelchair."[1]

What follows is a moving moment in television history—one that has been celebrated in books, documentaries, and articles. We watch a respectful adult truly engage with a charming child who happens to face significant physical challenges.

Jeffrey demonstrates his wheelchair, to Rogers's evident delight. "Jeff, your mom and dad must be really proud of you," he says. "I know I am."

Jeffrey matter-of-factly discusses his condition and his Madison doctors, concluding, "This just shows that you have a lot of things happening to you when you're handicapped." Rogers responds with encouragement: "Of course, but you're able to talk about those things so well. And help other people who might have the same kinds of things."

Rogers asks Jeffrey to join him in a rendition of "It's You I Like." Looking into each other's eyes, they sing the affectionate lyrics: "I hope that you'll remember, even when you're feeling blue, that it's you I like."

Fred bids farewell to Jeffrey with a valuable message for young viewers: "We have to all discover our own ways, don't we, of doing things when we're feeling blue." He adds, laughing, "I'm not feeling blue right now, though!"

"Me neither!" Jeffrey answers, a beatific smile indicating that one of his dreams has just come true.

In the 1990s, Erlanger graduated from Madison's Edgewood College with a degree in political science and embarked on the career Mister Rogers envisioned for him: helping other people with disabilities. He devoted himself to public service, chairing Madison's Commission on People with Disabilities and pushing for accessible taxi service, among other innovations. His work earned him a commendation from the US Senate, and the city of Madison later established the Jeffrey Clay Erlanger Civility in Public Discourse Award. Erlanger inspired people with a glass-half-full motto: "It doesn't matter what I *can't* do. It's what I *can* do. That's how I try to live my life."[2]

Rogers considered Jeffrey's appearance on *Mister Rogers'*

Neighborhood an all-time highlight. He often referred to it in speeches as a way of motivating people to overcome their own obstacles.

Erlanger died in 2007, at just thirty-six, and his motto continues to inspire passersby on his tombstone in Madison's Forest Hill Cemetery. If his death makes you feel a bit blue, I encourage you to watch the video of his last encounter with Fred Rogers at 1999's Academy of Television Arts & Sciences Awards. During a segment honoring Rogers, Erlanger rolled onto the stage in a tuxedo, treating his friend to an emotional surprise. Fred could barely hold back his tears as Jeffrey said, "When you tell people 'it's you I like,' we know that you really mean it. And tonight, I want you to know that, on behalf of millions of children and grownups, it's *you* that I like."[3]

Whenever I watch this euphoric clip, I can relate to Rogers's comment from that 1981 episode: "I'm not feeling blue right now!"

73

Joshua Glover

"Oh, I'm Not Afraid"

One early summer night in 1852, an enslaved Black man named Joshua escaped from Benammi Stone Garland's farm in St. Louis. A courageous journey of nearly four hundred miles by foot brought him to the city of Racine in the free state of Wisconsin. He chose the surname Glover and took a job at the Rice and Sinclair sawmill, where he earned a freeman's wage. After two years in Racine, he had become a respected member of the community—but back in St. Louis, Garland, fuming, got wind of Glover's whereabouts.

With the Fugitive Slave Act of 1850 on his side, Garland petitioned a federal court for a warrant to recapture Glover, even in a state where slavery was prohibited. Accompanied by two US marshals, he barged into Glover's Racine-area cabin and violently attacked him. The posse manacled Glover and drove him to the Milwaukee County jail—a quick pit stop on the way back to enslavement. Or so they thought.

It turned out that Garland had messed with the wrong state. Wisconsin abolitionists despised the Fugitive Slave Act and the equally pernicious Kansas–Nebraska Bill, which would allow slavery to expand into western territories. In Racine, word spread of Glover's kidnapping, and church bells rang to summon townsfolk to Haymarket Square. The largest assembled group in the city's history listened to fiery speeches defending the honor of "a faithful laborer and honest man."[1] Meanwhile, a committee formed to condemn the abduction and demand that Glover receive a fair trial. Committee members threw in a denunciation of the Fugitive Slave Act, declaring it hereby "repealed."

The committee telegraphed its resolutions to Sherman Booth, editor of Milwaukee's abolitionist newspaper the *Milwaukee Free Democrat*. Booth rode through Milwaukee, passing out handbills that asked, "Shall a man be dragged back to Slavery from our Free Soil, without an open trial of his right to liberty?"[2] Soon, a crowd of thousands followed him to the jail on the courthouse square, including a delegation from Racine. The Racine County sheriff flashed a warrant for Garland's arrest for assault and battery—a development that must have utterly astonished an enslaver accustomed to getting his way.

The protesters procured a writ of habeas corpus from a Milwaukee County judge, ordering due process for Glover. The federal officers refused to obey it. More fervent speeches followed, some delivered from a rooftop on the courthouse square. Booth suggested, in so many words, that the swelling crowd make their feelings known about the Fugitive Slave Act.

Which is exactly what they did.

Citizens demanded the keys to the jail. When refused, they fashioned a battering ram from a twenty-foot beam borrowed from a nearby construction site, broke down the door, and rescued the prisoner. Glover was carried down Wisconsin Street by his rescuers while handkerchiefs waved through open windows. At Walker's Point, he hopped into a waiting buggy, tipping his hat to the crowd and shouting "Glory hallelujah!" On the way to an Underground Railroad waystation west of Milwaukee, someone told Glover not to fear. "Oh, I'm not afraid," he responded, "not at all."[3]

Garland kept up the chase as Glover zoomed from one safe house to another over the next month, through Rochester and Burlington and finally back to Racine. There, abolitionists helped him secure passage to Canada, where he lived as a free man for the rest of his life.

Booth faced trial in 1854 for his role in Glover's escape, giving him another chance to heap scorn on the Fugitive Slave Act. "I rejoice that, in the first attempt of the slave-hunters to convert our jail into a slave-pen and our citizens into slave-catchers," he snarled in court, "they have signally failed, and that it has been decided by the spontaneous uprising and sovereign voice of the people, that no human being can be dragged into bondage from Milwaukee."[4]

The Wisconsin Supreme Court agreed with Booth and declared the Fugitive Slave Act unconstitutional, making Wisconsin the only state to take such action. The US Supreme Court, to its shame, rejected this decision and sentenced Booth to a fine and imprisonment.

But at least one enslaved person had secured his freedom. And only four million left to go.

74

Mildred Fish-Harnack

An American vs. Hitler

Photographs of young Mildred Fish-Harnack sometimes recall those of Anne Frank. Both portray high-spirited girls with carefree smiles enjoying everyday activities. It requires a stretch of the imagination to envision these ordinary kids in days to come, summoning exceptional courage to resist the Nazis.

Mildred Fish grew up in Milwaukee in the early 1900s, abhorring the local prejudice against her German neighbors. In high school, she joined a women's rights group. And at the University of Wisconsin in Madison, she engaged in intense political discussions with a circle of activist friends, debating everything from socialism to women's suffrage.

Along with politics, Fish loved the arts. She earned a bachelor's degree in humanities and a master's in English literature while writing poetry on the side. During a teaching stint at the UW, she met Arvid Harnack, an earnest doctoral student from Germany who stumbled into her class by mistake. The two spent time together hiking and canoeing on Lake Mendota, and despite the language barrier, they fell deeply in love. On a 1926 stroll through Picnic Point, one of campus's loveliest spots, they became engaged.

After their marriage, Mildred moved to Germany with Arvid and embarked on an academic and publishing career. The couple nurtured utopian dreams and believed the Soviet Union might hold the key to a just society. (Cue more intense political discussions with a new circle of activist friends.)

The topic of conversation changed in 1933 when Adolf Hitler came to power. In response to Nazi atrocities, Mildred and Arvid embarked on daring resistance activities with a group dubbed the Red Orchestra. They covertly distributed anti-Nazi literature, aided Jews, and gave their Allied contacts military secrets obtained in resistance circles. But in September 1942, disaster struck: arrest by the Gestapo, quickly followed by Arvid's execution.

The Nazis took photos of forty-year-old Mildred following her arrest. Gone was the carefree expression of her youth, replaced by a steely gaze and a determined set of the mouth. A kangaroo court initially sentenced her to six years in prison, but Hitler demanded her death. On February 16, 1943, Mildred Fish-Harnack became the only American woman executed on the dictator's direct orders.

At first, many in Wisconsin failed to recognize her heroism, put off by her communist sympathies. In 1986, however, the state established Mildred Fish-Harnack Day, and in 1994 UW–Madison instituted an annual Mildred Fish-Harnack Human Rights and Democracy Lecture. In 2019, the city of Madison erected a sculpture called *Mildred*, its slablike design patterned after an ancient stele.

On my first visit to this memorial, I shrugged at its blank abstraction. Why not a figurative sculpture to convey Fish-Harnack's resolute expression from those last photographs? But I've come to appreciate *Mildred*'s dignity and solidity as it rises proudly from Wisconsin soil, suggesting her unwavering resistance to tyranny. And the location can't be beat: the Lake Mendota shoreline facing Picnic Point, where Mildred and Arvid declared their eternal love.

75

Mountain Wolf Woman and
Nancy Oestreich Lurie

"How I Lived My Life"

In 1957, a unique cross-cultural collaboration took place between white anthropologist Nancy Oestreich Lurie and Mountain Wolf Woman, or Xéhachiwinga, a Ho-Chunk woman from Black River Falls. Lurie had immersed herself in Ho-Chunk culture as a student at the University of Wisconsin and grown so close to tribal member Mitchell Redcloud Senior that he adopted her as his daughter. Through this act, Mountain Wolf Woman became Lurie's aunt. The women developed a close bond and agreed to work together on Mountain Wolf Woman's autobiography. Anthropologists had previously recorded testimony from American Indian men—notably Crashing Thunder, who was Mountain Wolf Woman's brother—but this would be the rare full-length written account of a Native woman's life told from her point of view.

Mountain Wolf Woman, at age seventy-three, fully committed to the project by flying to Lurie's house in Ann Arbor, Michigan (the first flight of her lifetime), and moving in for a five-week series of tape recordings. She made herself at home by sewing clothing, splitting firewood, and preparing meals in Lurie's fireplace, which she preferred to the electric stove given her usual practice of cooking over an open fire. When the time came for Mountain Wolf Woman to record her interview, she folded her hands in her lap, closed her eyes, and told her life story in Ho-Chunk, chuckling at the funny parts and crying at the sad ones. The resulting book, 1961's *Mountain Wolf Woman, Sister of Crashing Thunder,* shows us just how it felt to trap muskrat, gather wild potatoes, and enjoy ceremonial dances in a turn-of-the-century Ho-Chunk community.

Mountain Wolf Woman was the last of six children—"poor quality, they used to say of that one," she joked.[1] A log house near Black River Falls served as her family's home base, but they ranged around the region with the seasons. Muskrat trapping occurred in spring, by the Mississippi River near La Crosse. In the fall, they hunted deer near Neillsville while living in a cattail wigwam. "Thus the Indians came through history," she said, proud of her community's survival skills.

Mountain Wolf Woman excelled at using sensory details to bring scenes to life, such as the process of gathering yellow water lily roots. She and other women took off their shoes, waded into a slough, and felt for the roots with their bare feet. Then they dug them out with their toes, allowing the roots to float up to the surface. Back at home, they scraped the roots, strung up the slices to dry, and later cooked them with meat in a savory concoction. "Whatever the situation," she observed, "[Indians] always found something to do and were able to obtain food for themselves by such methods. Whatever the circumstances, the Indian is always doing something useful."

Mountain Wolf Woman did not style her tale as a dramatic hero's journey, the way Crashing Thunder did. And yet, as she described her coming of age, her heroic qualities became apparent. She left an abusive husband she'd been forced to marry. Even with scant resources, she fed her children and cared for needy elders. She raised her grandchildren in troubled times. And, perhaps most impressive, she preserved her cherished traditions while navigating a region increasingly dominated by white immigrants. "Whatever is good," she said, "that I would do."

Born in Milwaukee in 1924, Nancy Oestreich Lurie was impressive in her own right. Before her collaboration with Mountain Wolf

More than fifty years after this studio portrait was taken,
Mountain Wolf Woman recounted her dramatic life
story to anthropologist Nancy Oestreich Lurie for a
landmark book. WHI IMAGE ID 9385

Woman, she taught at the University of Wisconsin–Milwaukee and
the University of Michigan; afterward, she served as curator of
anthropology at the Milwaukee Public Museum and became a
leading figure in the field of ethnohistory. She also advocated for
the Ojibwe, Menominee, and other Native nations as an expert witness when they brought land claims before state and federal courts.

In *Mountain Wolf Woman, Sister of Crashing Thunder,* Lurie provided a model for bridging the gap between Indigenous people and
the white Americans who have historically mistreated and

misunderstood them. With its affectionate preface, conscientious notes, and thoughtful approach to the interview process, the book is a concerted effort to respectfully tell this important story.

In return, Mountain Wolf Woman did Lurie the honor of making her part of the tale. As she ended her testimony, she noted the researcher's kindness toward Native people and her sincere interest in their history. "That is why I am here, saying this at her home," Mountain Wolf Woman concluded. "I even rode in an airplane, and I came here. And here I am, telling in [Ho-Chunk] how I lived my life."

76

Hans Christian Heg

Another of Our Best and Bravest

As the Civil War raged in September 1863, the *Wisconsin State Journal* printed this heartbreaking bulletin: "The painful rumor that Col. Hans Christian Heg, of the 15th Wisconsin, was among the slain at Chickamauga is confirmed. Thus is added another of our best and bravest to the victims of this accursed rebellion."[1]

The Scandinavian American hero was gone but not forgotten. Statues of Heg were erected at the Capitol in Madison and in the town of Norway, and a Wind Lake park was named in his honor. Outside the state, he was celebrated with a monument at Chickamauga and Chattanooga National Military Park, a World War II–era ship in his name, and a statue in his birthplace of Lier, Norway. Though Heg walked the earth for just thirty-three years, the values he lived by and died for continue to inspire people around the world.

When Hans was eleven in 1840, his family joined a wave of Norwegian immigration to Wisconsin. They settled in Muskego, bought a farm, and built a large barn that served as a waystation for other Norwegians seeking homes in the state. Young Hans not only mastered English but also absorbed the American tenets of freedom and equality. As a teenager, he wholeheartedly joined the antislavery movement, working for the Free Soil Party.

In 1859, after Wisconsinites elected Heg as state prison commissioner on the Republican ticket, he embarked on a series of humane reforms from Waupun. But his promising political career ended when Southern states seceded from the Union in 1861. Even with a wife and three children back on the farm, Heg knew where his duty lay. "The government of our adopted country is in danger," he wrote to his fellow Scandinavian Americans. "That which we learned to love as freemen in our old Fatherland—our government—our independence—is threatened with destruction. Is it not our duty as brave and intelligent citizens to extend our hands in defense of the cause of our country and of our own homes?"[2]

In October 1861, Heg received a commission as colonel and set about raising a regional Scandinavian regiment, the mighty Fifteenth. A newspaper editorial hailed him as "honorable, unimpeachably honest, to a high degree considerate of the welfare of his subordinates, with a splendid fund of practical, sound sense." The editors went so far as to call Heg "the best man of all the Norwegians whom we know of in America to lead such an undertaking."[3]

Heg directed the Fifteenth—including regimental companies dubbed Odin's Rifles and Norway Bear Hunters—in gruesome engagements in Kentucky, Tennessee, and Georgia. The soldiers admired his bravery as he led the charge on the front lines with a spirited wave of his hat. Even after taking a bullet to the gut at the dreadful battle of Chickamauga, he rallied the troops and rode for another quarter mile before collapsing from loss of blood.

In his last moments, on September 20, 1863, Heg expressed his willingness to die for a just cause. He would surely have celebrated the emancipation of enslaved Black people at the war's end.

In an unfortunate twist of fate, this man who sacrificed all for abolition was, literally, dragged through the mud in Madison. In a 2020 antiracist protest precipitated by the murder of George Floyd, demonstrators puzzlingly pulled down Heg's statue, decapitated it, and threw it into Lake Monona. Within a month, the state began raising funds for the statue's repair and, one year later, restored it to a place of honor at the Capitol. A century and a half after Heg's death, Wisconsin residents proudly reaffirmed that his devotion to freedom and equality is worth remembering forever.

77

Laurel Clark

Interstellar Dreamer

Astronaut Laurel Clark's life ended abruptly on February 1, 2003, when the space shuttle *Columbia* exploded near the end of its mission. She was only forty-one, with a husband and an eight-year-old son. It's poignant to see photographs of Clark smiling during her mission as she poses with crewmates or floats through the cabin in her orange spacesuit. For a woman who'd only recently envisioned herself in space, the *Columbia* experience seemed like a dream come true.

Laurel was a self-described boring straight-A student at Racine's Horlick High School in the late 1970s. She earned a bachelor's degree in zoology and a medical degree from the University of Wisconsin–Madison, where she blossomed intellectually. "It was a wonderful place that expected excellence and emphasized independence," she said. "It was an environment that really taught me to think on my own."[1]

As it turned out, her life proved to be anything but boring. She joined the US Navy and served as an undersea medical officer and flight surgeon. After marrying fellow navy officer Jonathan Clark, she tried her hand at parachuting, rock climbing, and scuba diving. In her thirties, and on the lookout for the next challenge, she got the idea of becoming an astronaut. The space program turned her down on the first try but accepted her on the second—while she was pregnant, no less.

Family and friends recognized her unique character. They knew she would follow her own path, no matter the risk, and that she would enjoy herself in the process. "There's a lot of different things that we do during life that could potentially harm us," she told an interviewer, "and I choose not to stop doing those things."[2]

In space, Clark conducted experiments on moths, roses, and gravity. Nearly two hundred miles above the Earth, she also maintained her ties to Wisconsin. Two of her in-flight experiments originated at the UW's Wisconsin Center for Space Automation and Robotics. Her gear included a UW medical school medallion and a Wisconsin-made teddy bear with *UW–Madison* and *Zoology* embroidered on its jacket. In a preflight interview, she said, "I really haven't been able to visit Madison as much as I would like to. . . . I'm actually very much looking forward to coming back and sharing with people there some of the places I've been and some of the things I've done."[3]

Surely that would have been an inspiring talk. For fifteen days, twenty-two hours, and twenty minutes, Clark reveled in the wonders of spaceflight. In an email to the folks back home, she described her view from the porthole. "I have seen some incredible sights: lightning spreading over the Pacific, the Aurora Australis lighting up the entire visible horizon with the cityglow of Australia below, the crescent moon setting over the limb of the Earth, the vast plains of Africa and the dunes on Cape Horn, rivers breaking through tall mountain passes."[4] She was especially happy to get a glimpse of the Wind Point peninsula jutting into Lake Michigan near her childhood home in Racine.

Minutes before *Columbia* disintegrated, due to a damaged wing, Clark remained in high spirits. The astronauts, unaware of the malfunction, joked around as she filmed them with a digital camera. After encouraging flight engineer Kalpana Chawla to wave, Clark turned the camera on herself to provide one final image for posterity.

It was a smile.

78

Abraham Lincoln

A Modest Man in Stocking Feet

I'm fascinated by Abraham Lincoln's journey from self-educated rail-splitter to author of the Emancipation Proclamation, and I'll go anywhere to walk in his footsteps. I've driven to his out-of-the-way boyhood homes in Kentucky and Indiana. I've followed him to the White House and Ford's Theater in Washington, DC. And I've explored every touchstone in his home state of Illinois, no matter how obscure. In the small town of Petersburg, I tramped through a farmer's field to a forgotten pioneer cemetery, climbed over a rusty fence, and located the tombstone for Ann Rutledge. Yes, I was technically trespassing, but I just had to see the spot where Lincoln wept over his first love's grave.

You'd think, as someone so obsessed with Lincoln, I would have visited the one site less than an hour from my home in Madison. But I hadn't heard of Honest Abe's connection to Janesville until I happened to read about it at a highway rest stop. Turns out, I'd sped past a Lincoln shrine dozens of times on Interstate 90 without realizing it.

In 1859, Abe visited Wisconsin to warm up for his first presidential campaign. He gave a speech in Milwaukee and then one in Beloit, where he met fellow Republican William Tallman. Tallman invited the politician to speak in nearby Janesville and then spend a Saturday night with his family. Lincoln gladly accepted the spontaneous offer.

The Tallmans, who lived in a mansion overlooking the Rock River, planned to kick a less distinguished visitor out of their guest room so Lincoln could have it to himself. But Abe would hear none of that. Humble as ever, he insisted on sharing the room (which also meant sharing the bed) with his fellow guest.

At the time, people customarily left boots outside their doors on Saturday nights so they could be cleaned by servants and returned in the morning. But when Lincoln woke up the next day, his boots had not reappeared by the door. He felt too embarrassed to come to breakfast in his stocking feet, so he stayed in his room. His sense of decency caused him to miss the train back to Illinois.

The Tallmans found the boots and apologized. Lincoln, who suddenly had time on his hands, worshipped with the family down the hill at Janesville's First Congregational Church. He picnicked with them under one of their impressive oak trees, slept over Sunday night, and finally caught his train home the following day.

The Tallman residence is now known as the Lincoln Tallman House. The Rock County Historical Society conducts tours of the property (including the still-standing oak tree), proud of Janesville's encounter with an American icon. True, Lincoln spent just two nights there, but that was enough to put his stamp on the place. After all, what's more Lincolnesque than refusing special treatment? Or missing a train due to excessive modesty?

In other words, there's no need to leave Wisconsin to commune with Abraham Lincoln. And no need for me to climb over any more rusty graveyard fences in Illinois.

79

Ada Deer

"I Fight Back!"

From an early age, Ada Deer knew how profoundly Native people across North America suffered from their loss of land and dignity. Her Menominee father was forced to attend a boarding school that sought to extinguish American Indian culture, and the experience scarred him. Her white mother, meanwhile, encouraged activism. "You were put on this earth for a purpose," Ma Deer told Ada. "You are here to help people. You are here to help your people."[1]

Like many Wisconsin residents in the 1930s and '40s, Ada grew up with no electricity or indoor plumbing. She didn't necessarily mind walking from her home on the Menominee Reservation to the local hospital for a bath or hauling up water from the Wolf River to wash her clothes. What she did mind was anything that took time away from reading. She loved learning about tribal history and attended meetings of the all-male Menominee Indian Advisory Council, diligently taking notes. The bookish girl with the long braids and glasses came to appreciate her membership in a sovereign Indian nation.

After attending college at the University of Wisconsin and Columbia University, Deer helped create an advocacy group—Determination of Rights and Unity for Menominee Shareholders, or DRUMS—that challenged the federal policy of termination. With the Menominee Termination Act of 1954, the government had abrogated the treaty that established the Menominee Reservation and the tribe's sovereignty. In other words, the rights that the Menominee had been coerced into accepting in exchange for their

Ada Deer was a driving force behind 1973's Menominee Restoration Act, which helped a wronged Native nation reclaim its rights. UNIVERSITY OF WISCONSIN-MADISON ARCHIVES

land disappeared. The result was an end to self-governance, leading to poverty and despair.

In 1970, DRUMS sought to restore the Menominee's sovereign status and reclaim their resources. That meant sending somebody to Washington, DC, to lobby members of Congress. "Who's going to Washington?" Deer asked at a DRUMS meeting. No one volunteered, so off she went to do it herself.[2]

Deer was a social worker and knew how to bring people around to her point of view. And she was not afraid to confront the racists in the US government. Her efforts contributed to the passage of 1973's Menominee Restoration Act, which reestablished the nation as sovereign and federally recognized. That massive accomplishment was a prelude to 1975's Indian Self-Determination and Education Act, 1978's Indian Child Welfare Act, and 1978's American Indian Religious Freedom Act. Such was the power of one small Wisconsin tribe—and one determined woman.

Deer went on to serve as assistant secretary of the interior for Indian affairs in the Clinton administration, and she shaped federal Indian policy by serving on countless other committees and commissions. To appreciate her indomitable spirit, picture Deer walking in DC one night when two muggers ran off with her purse. Instead of letting them go, she chased the assailants for several blocks, yelling, until they boarded a passing bus. Then she flagged down a police car, jumped in, and took off after them. Needless to say, the muggers had little chance against this brave soul. The cops caught up with the bus, and Deer strolled home with her purse.

She later described the mindset that drove her that night—indeed, that drove her for a lifetime: "I don't let people walk on me. I fight back!"[3]

80

Caroline Quarlls

The Great Escape

In 1842, sixteen-year-old Caroline Quarlls was enslaved in St. Louis by Mrs. Charles Hall. She decided she'd had enough when Hall grabbed her in a fit of rage and forcibly cut off her hair. Quarlls gathered her things and stole away on the Fourth of July—a good day for declaring freedom from tyranny.

She managed to cross the Mississippi River on a steamboat and board a stagecoach in Illinois. Fortunately, it was headed north to Wisconsin—a free state with a devoted antislavery contingent. But a St. Louis posse trailed her all the way to Milwaukee, waving wads of cash for information on her whereabouts.

The local network of white abolitionists, however, could not be bought off. And with their help, Quarlls made one of the greatest escapes in US history.

She embarked on a harrowing journey through eastern Wisconsin's Underground Railroad, traveling from Milwaukee to Lisbon to Spring Prairie to Prairieville (now known as Waukesha). Along the way, she hid in a sugar barrel, under mounds of hay, and in a potato chute. Her allies lied on her behalf, stalled for time, and refused to cooperate when the pursuers confronted them. In one instance, a lawyer with a warrant shouted at the abolitionist Ezra Mendall, "You are harboring that slave-girl, which is against the law!" According to Michael Edmonds and Samantha Snyder's *Warriors, Saints, and Scoundrels*, Mendall retorted, "Well, a bad law is sometimes better broken than obeyed."[1]

Prairieville farmer Lyman Goodnow volunteered to take Quarlls to Canada, beyond the reach of her tormentors. With a borrowed horse and buggy and a pillowcase full of donated food, the two set off on the treacherous six-hundred-mile trek. Three weeks later, when Lyman dropped Quarlls at a missionary's house in Sandwich, Canada, she bid him farewell as her "dearest friend."

Goodnow rode back to his farm, where neighbors had taken care of the harvest for him. The pursuers returned to St. Louis emptyhanded. Quarlls found work on a Canada farm, married, had children, and learned to read and write. In fact, thirty-eight years after her Wisconsin odyssey, she wrote a letter to Goodnow in response to one she'd received from him.

"I am still in Sandwich the same place where you left me," she wrote. "Just as soon as the postmaster read to me—your name—my heart was filled with joy and gladness and I should like to see you once more before I die to return you thanks for your kindness towards me."

Quarlls signed off just as she had in 1842, pledging eternal gratitude to her "dearest friend."[2]

81

Edward Berner, George Hallauer, and the Girl from Two Rivers

Inventing the Ice Cream Sundae

A Wisconsin State Historical Marker claims Two Rivers as the birthplace of my favorite dessert, the ice cream sundae. Did a major worldwide phenomenon really originate in this modest city?

According to the marker, a local man named George Hallauer strolled into a soda fountain on Fifteenth Street in 1881. He asked owner Edward Berner to top a dish of ice cream with chocolate sauce, a substance previously reserved for ice cream sodas. The new concoction caught on around town, and Berner began selling it for a nickel—but just on Sundays.

Enter the story's third hero, an anonymous ten-year-old girl who insisted on having a dish of ice cream "with that stuff on top" on a different day of the week. That was a nonstarter for Berner— until the girl cleverly suggested that they "pretend it was Sunday." That opened the floodgates, with the shopkeeper offering the dish every day in many flavors.

The unusual spelling of "sundae" reportedly started when a glassware salesman placed an order for the canoe-shaped dishes Berner used. He requested "sundae dishes" with an *e* at the end rather than a *y*, and the rest is history. Or so says the state of Wisconsin.

On a 2018 trip to Two Rivers, I wondered if this origin story held up. I searched for "first ice cream sundae" on my cellphone and found that, sure enough, Two Rivers has rivals to the claim, including nearby Manitowoc. The most aggressive challenger is Ithaca, New York, which points to an 1892 newspaper ad for a locally served sundae. In a 2006 *New York Times* article on the dispute, Ithaca's mayor haughtily claimed: "We have the historical documents and they don't."[1]

Two Rivers did not take that insult lying down. The city passed a resolution demanding that Ithaca cease and desist with its sundae slanders. Townsfolk also deluged Ithaca's mayor with postcards featuring the Two Rivers historical marker. On matters of milk fat, Ithaca learned, you cross the Dairy State at your peril.

So, what's the truth? To gather crucial evidence, I walked into the Two Rivers visitor center in an 1850s inn. You can bet the complex housed a soda fountain, named for none other than Edward Berner. Purely for the sake of historical research, I ordered an ice cream sundae. Was it a descendant of the world's first sundae, served here in 1881? Sorry, Ithaca, I have no documentation. All I'll say is that, with its thick chocolate sauce, overflowing whipped cream, and juicy cherry on top, the dish made me a believer.

82

Kathryn Clarenbach

Turning Antagonists into Allies

Since the mid-1800s, women's movements in the United States have had no shortage of visionaries, from Elizabeth Cady Stanton to Sojourner Truth to Betty Friedan. But they have also needed competent organizers, and that's the role Kathryn Clarenbach played beginning in the 1960s. She was born in 1920 and grew up a Methodist minister's daughter in Sparta, inspired by her mother's activism as a school board member. Her parents admired female achievers and took young Kay to see pioneering aviator Amelia Earhart and celebrity preacher Aimee Semple McPherson. No surprise—she became an achiever herself.

As a University of Wisconsin student in the late 1930s, Clarenbach abhorred the prohibition against women in the student union's Rathskeller, so she walked s-l-o-w-l-y through the male-only space to make a point. After obtaining a PhD at the UW, she was hired as a faculty member but earned a fraction of what her male colleagues did.

Seeing unfairness all around her, Clarenbach spurred the creation of a statewide Governor's Commission on the Status of Women and became its first chairwoman. During the fifteen years she served as chair, the commission challenged scores of laws that discriminated against women, and Clarenbach traveled the state to explain its work to sometimes skeptical Wisconsinites. She was known for treating her audiences with respect and turning antagonists into allies—a version of "Wisconsin nice," here turned to radical ends.

Clarenbach worked well within the system, but by 1966, she

realized the federal government would not seriously address discrimination against women without a kick in the pants. At a gathering that year in Washington, DC, she and a couple dozen
collaborators—including Betty Friedan, author of *The Feminine
Mystique*—hatched the idea of the National Organization for
Women (NOW). Clarenbach collected five-dollar donations from
those present, saved the napkin that laid out the organization's
founding principles, and became its first chairwoman. For the
next six years, her UW office in Madison essentially served as
NOW's headquarters.

The combative Friedan had big ideas but no organizational
experience, so Clarenbach took on the job of making things work.
While the press often ridiculed NOW, and much of the public
initially viewed it as too extreme, she used her diplomatic skills
to forge alliances with mainstream women's organizations. And
so emerged a potent movement. NOW pressured the government
and corporations for equal rights in employment and public
accommodations—and got results. The group deserves some of the
credit for passage of 1972's Title IX, which guaranteed women equal
educational opportunities.

"Kay was the foremost organizer of the modern women's movement, recognized as such by all who worked with her... the reliable,
sustaining force without which there is no social change," said
UW–Madison historian Gerda Lerner.[1]

Throughout the 1970s, Clarenbach's brand of civility paid off in
success after success. She became the founding chairwoman of the
National Women's Political Caucus, which increased the number of
women elected and appointed to office. She also coordinated 1977's
momentous National Women's Conference, which drew twenty
thousand attendees and confirmed that the fight for women's rights
was picking up steam.

Rarely has "Wisconsin nice" been so ferociously effective.

83

Ada James

The Equality Club

Can you change the world from a small Wisconsin town? Ada James proved it's possible, given the right mixture of passion and planning.

Richland Center had about a thousand residents when James was born there in 1876, the daughter of two progressive political activists. Her father served as a state senator, and her mother founded the Richland Center Woman's Club, the first group in the state to work for women's right to vote. That earned Richland Center a visit in 1886 from none other than suffrage superstar Susan B. Anthony.

With such role models, James had no intention of conforming to the era's traditional notions of femininity. In high school, she cofounded the Equality Club to advance women's suffrage. As a young woman, she broke off an engagement when she realized her fiancé expected a stay-at-home wife. Instead, she redoubled her political activities as vice president of the Wisconsin Woman Suffrage Association. But even this group proved too conservative for the increasingly radical firebrand.

In 1911, James cofounded the Political Equality League of Wisconsin to work on a statewide referendum for women's suffrage. She employed scandalous tactics, such as sending women on pro-suffrage automobile tours. She also used a newfangled contraption called an airplane to drop brochures.

James faced formidable opposition: brewing interests that spent big to prevent women from gaining the vote and, they assumed, supporting temperance. The referendum lost in a landslide, but

James didn't relent—she recalibrated. She joined forces with the militant rebels in the Congressional Union for Woman Suffrage, later known as the National Woman's Party, and organized a Wisconsin chapter. This group played hardball. Members picketed the White House, endured brutal stints in prison, and staged hunger strikes. Their goal was the passage of a national law to ensure women's right to vote.

James reluctantly missed the White House demonstrations, duty bound to stay with her aging father in Richland Center. But she played a key role in the movement after both houses of Congress finally passed a constitutional amendment for women's suffrage. For the amendment to become law, three-fourths of the states had to ratify it—no easy task. James led the charge in Wisconsin, which became the first state to ratify on June 10, 1919. One year later, women secured the national right to vote with the Nineteenth Amendment to the Constitution, a testament to decades of intense lobbying by James and her colleagues.

What a difference you can make from a small Wisconsin town.

84

Electa Quinney

A Teacher to Remember

In 2023 Kaukauna, I found few traces of the Stockbridge Indian village that once existed there. The people who now call themselves the Stockbridge-Munsee Band of Mohican Indians came to the area from the East Coast in the 1820s—one of many moves the tribe had made over the preceding century due to pressures from white settlers and the coercive tactics of the federal government. They left for a reservation in Calumet County in the 1830s following treaty negotiations, and their log houses south of the Fox River have given way to gas stations and convenience stores. But Kaukauna—along with Wisconsin and the world—still remembers Stockbridge-Munsee Band member Electa Quinney, the smart, kind, well-educated woman who served as the state's first public schoolteacher.

Electa was born in New York State in 1802, a time when the Mohican tribe (later called the Stockbridge) had begun to modify their traditional ways after the arrival of Europeans. Like many other Mohicans, she attended school with white students, learning to read and write English as well as studying math, geography, astronomy, and Christianity. She taught school in New York for six years and moved to Wisconsin with the rest of the tribe in 1828. Her skills made her the natural choice for a teacher in the new settlement.

According to Karyn Saemann's *Electa Quinney: Stockbridge Teacher*, she taught Native children in the log building that also served as the community's church, starting each day with a prayer. This was Wisconsin's first public school, supported by funds from tribal members. Within a few months, the children of white missionaries began attending classes as well, to learn spelling, reading, public speaking, and math.

Later, Quinney taught school in nearby Smithfield and Duck Creek, receiving—as we'd say today—good reviews. One missionary called her "a person of good education" and "very faithful to the children." A student later compared her classroom to "the best public schools of New England."[1] Other surviving testimony characterizes her as compassionate, intelligent, pious, and dignified. Tall, too.

Quinney married a Mohawk man named Daniel Adams in 1833. They moved to an area in what's now Missouri and had three sons. Two decades later, she returned to Wisconsin for good and lived on a farm in the town of Stockbridge. Though she was long past her career in education, people remembered her as "the schoolteacher."

On my stroll through Kaukauna, I passed a brick church with a tall spire that would have towered over the log version from Quinney's day. I stopped in Thelen Park to read a Wisconsin State Historical Marker about Hendrick Aupaumut and Jacob Konkapot, Stockbridge Indians who served in the Revolutionary War and were buried nearby. Finally, heading south toward the bulbous Kaukauna water tower, I came upon a modern brick building with carloads of children streaming out of the parking lot.

A sign at the entrance identified it as Electa Quinney Elementary School.

85

Vel Phillips

Doing the Right Thing

In 1956, Vel Phillips became the first woman and the first Black person to serve on Milwaukee's city council. Her fellow council members made no secret of their disapproval and declined to share an office with her. And they panicked when she walked into the sole restroom in council chambers, putting up a Men Only sign—with *Only* italicized. Phillips insisted on her right to use the restroom, and a city attorney's ruling backed her up.

This was Phillips's standard operating procedure: bursting through doors that normally slammed shut on women and Black people.

Her barrier-breaking ways began in the 1940s at Milwaukee's North Division High School, where she fought to get into the college prep classes denied to Black students. A racist judge blocked her path in an oratorical contest, but a petition drive reversed the ruling. She won the contest, and her rhetorical skills earned her a full scholarship to Howard University.

In 1951, Phillips became the first Black woman to graduate from the University of Wisconsin Law School, then moved back to Milwaukee to put her legal know-how to use in the fight against discrimination. As the first Black person elected to the Democratic Party's national committee in 1958, she stood up to Southern segregationists. When Florida senator Spessard Holland insisted that Democrats would lose the 1960 presidential election by advocating for civil rights, she retorted, "Winning isn't nearly so important as doing the right thing."[1]

Vel Phillips, pictured in 1979 during her
tenure as Wisconsin's secretary of state,
broke through one barrier after another.
WHI IMAGE ID 55022

On the Milwaukee city council, Phillips turned her attention to housing practices that enforced segregation and restricted Black residents to the central city. She introduced her fair housing ordinance in 1962 and got no support from her eighteen white colleagues. The law went nowhere for the next five years, with Phillips regularly reintroducing it. In 1967, supporters of fair housing commenced two hundred consecutive nights of protest marches, facing racist mobs that threw rocks and firecrackers at them. Someone shot a bullet through Phillips's window and left a note saying, "Go back to Africa."[2]

But she stood her ground, even spending a night in jail in defiance of the city's ban on marching. In 1968, amid racial justice protests throughout the country, the council passed a fair housing ordinance that Phillips supported. "I think it's a pretty great day for the city," she said, taking her place as a national civil rights legend.[3]

But there were still more "no entry" signs to breeze past. In 1971, she became the first Black person to serve as a Wisconsin judge. She also became the country's first Black woman elected to statewide executive office when she won her 1978 race for secretary of state. During her term, both the governor and lieutenant governor briefly left Wisconsin, providing her with yet another first for a woman and a Black person in the state: acting governor. She quipped that the men hurried back when they realized they'd left a woman in charge.

By the time Phillips died in 2018, the state where she had once been jailed had fully claimed her as a hero. Wisconsin now has schools, streets, and college dormitories in her name, along with a statue of her at the Capitol. The statue broke yet another barrier: it was the first commemoration of a Black leader on the Capitol grounds.

Near the end of her life, Phillips was able to enjoy one of her favorite tributes: a frozen-custard flavor at Bella's Fat Cat in Milwaukee called the Vel Phillips Special, which mixed chocolate and vanilla. "Kind of like black and white working together," she noted with pleasure.[4]

86

Belle Case La Follette

A Brainy and Conscientious Woman

Robert La Follette needs no introduction for those familiar with Wisconsin history. Beginning in the late nineteenth century, "Fightin' Bob" worked for progressive causes as an incorruptible US representative, US senator, governor, and presidential candidate. In roof-rattling speeches, he stood up for workers' rights, racial equality, economic fairness, women's suffrage, and civil liberties.

Unfortunately, Belle Case La Follette *does* need an introduction, even in her home state. Though Belle worked side by side with her famous husband, battling racists and reactionaries—her nickname could have been "Fightin'," too—she is woefully underappreciated. I'd say she deserves her own bust in the Wisconsin Capitol for matching Bob's heroics while facing an additional obstacle: second-class citizenship. As a woman, she couldn't even vote until 1920, at the age of sixty-one.

Belle was born in Primrose, grew up in Baraboo, and questioned sexist traditions from an early age. Her mother served as a role model, working equally with her husband on the family farm. With her parents' support, Belle entered the mostly male University of Wisconsin in 1875 as a go-getter who won speaking competitions and academic honors. Contrast her college career with that of classmate Bob La Follette, who struggled with assignments and seemed unlikely even to graduate.

And yet, Bob was smart enough to recognize a catch. He noted Belle's idealism and independence and fell hard. She kept him at arm's length romantically, regarding him more as a friend who shared her interest in oratory and public service. After graduation, she headed to Spring Green and then Baraboo for a career in education, with Bob in hot pursuit. When he proposed, she actually broke out laughing, but Belle ultimately warmed to the ambitious fellow with mutton-chops and wavy hair. She agreed to a marriage in 1881 with one stipulation: no mention of "obey" in the wedding vows.

Thus began a crucial partnership. Belle went on to become the first female graduate of the University of Wisconsin Law School and served as Bob's legal adviser when

As a heroic orator, activist, and journalist, Belle Case La Follette—pictured circa 1924—challenged her era's prejudices. WHI IMAGE ID 55358

he launched his political career. He called her his "wisest and best counselor" and tried to live up to her high standards.[1] She helped write his speeches and shape his progressive ideas. "There is no one in the world better fitted to be in politics than a brainy and conscientious woman," Bob said, "and there isn't a brainier woman in the country than my wife."[2]

This was a woman who wouldn't stay in the shadows. She became a public figure in her own right as an orator, activist, and journalist, challenging her era's prejudices. White supremacists lambasted her opposition to segregation. Warmongers sneered at the Woman's Peace Party, which she cofounded in 1915 in response to World War I. President Woodrow Wilson balked when she and others met with him about women's right to vote. Refusing to take no for an answer, Belle spoke out tirelessly in support of women's suffrage and exulted in the US Capitol gallery in 1919 when the Senate finally approved the Nineteenth Amendment. No less a suffragist than Alice Paul called her "the most consistent supporter of equal rights of all the women of her time."[3]

After Bob's death in 1925, Belle took over the family's magazine, *La Follette's Weekly* (later called *The Progressive*), and became an outspoken champion of American Indian rights. But she rejected a chance to assume Bob's US Senate seat, despite an urgent petition from Wisconsin residents that asked: "Will you, can you, turn away from your heritage, your people, your shepherdless flock?"[4]

She could and did, as she considered the offer more a tribute to Bob than a recognition of her own political potential. Nevertheless, when Belle died in 1931, the *New York Times* called her "the most influential of all American women who had to do with public affairs in this country."[5]

Isn't it time to install that bust of her at the Wisconsin Capitol?

87

Jesus Salas

"Let's Speak to Be Heard"

Jesus Salas comes from a family of Mexican American migrant workers who stuck up for their rights, even when it cost them dearly. In the early twentieth century, white authorities in Texas used a poll tax to keep Mexican Americans from voting, but Jesus's father and grandfather paid the fee from their meager funds. That's how badly they wanted to participate in the democratic process.

Jesus inherited their fortitude. The budding activist traveled with his family between backbreaking agricultural jobs in Mississippi, Illinois, and Wisconsin. As early as age seven, he worked in the fields with a child-size hoe. At times, his family of eight lived together in one-room shacks or slept in their vehicle. In a Hartford migrant camp, Jesus recalled, they at least had hot showers—but no privacy in the communal bathroom.

Jesus's father valued education and made sure he attended school wherever they lived. In his freshman year alone, Jesus went to three high schools as the family relocated in pursuit of work. Finally, in the early 1960s, his family left the migrant life and settled in Wautoma, shivering through the winter without warm clothes. That's where Jesus, at seventeen, found work enrolling migrant kids in a childcare program. So began his career as a changemaker.

At every migrant camp he visited, workers told Salas of troubles with their employers. He heard, "Someone got hurt." And "We didn't get paid."[1] He read a newspaper article about Cesar Chavez's campaign to organize migrant workers in California and promptly called him for advice. That led to Salas's idea of organizing a march from Wautoma to Madison in 1966. He purposely left the date, time, and meeting place off posters advertising the event, lest the authorities try to thwart it. Instead, the posters simply read, in Spanish, "Let's Get Together to Be Recognized. Let's Speak to Be Heard. Our People Have a Cause." Workers felt a surge of hope, and the details about where and when they would march spread by word of mouth.

The demonstration launched Obreros Unidos, or United Workers, a group Salas cofounded to unionize the migrant workers despite stiff opposition from growers. They took on no less a multinational giant than Libby's food company, employing walkouts, strikes, boycotts, and other nonviolent tactics inspired by Martin Luther King Jr. and Mahatma Gandhi. Given the opposition's seemingly limitless power, the effort required courage, conviction, and creativity. Barred from entering company-owned labor camps, the organizers staged migrant worker baseball tournaments where they could pass out buttons and pamphlets. They also established a newspaper, a gas co-op, a health center, and a legal-aid office to help migrants help themselves. When the time came to decide on a union, 98 percent of Libby's workers voted in favor.

As the organizing continued, Salas and his colleagues started the practice of having fiestas after their demonstrations. They were determined not only to fight but also to have fun.

By the late '60s, Salas was rivaling his hero Chavez as a nationally recognized advocate for Latino rights. As the director of Milwaukee's United Migrant Opportunity Services, he launched voter registration campaigns and supported the first Latino candidate for state office. He led a movement for Latino access to the University of Wisconsin–Milwaukee, bilingual education in Milwaukee schools, and a Chicano studies program at the University of Wisconsin–Madison.

The onetime rebel grew into a respected elder and earned a 2003 appointment to the University of Wisconsin System Board of Regents. Even as an insider, however, Salas has devoted himself to the fight for equal rights.

And you can bet he has fun doing so.

88

Marianne Labuche

Practicing the Healing Arts

Documentation is scarce for Marianne Labuche, often credited as Wisconsin's first doctor. But I'm grateful that we know about her at all. A key written record comes from her Prairie du Chien neighbor James Lockwood, who provides a single intriguing paragraph in his 1856 recollection, *Early Times and Events in Wisconsin.*

Lockwood describes Labuche—who was also called Mary Ann Menard—as having "mixed African and white blood." At the end of the eighteenth century, she traveled from the St. Louis area to Prairie du Chien, which was then a remote fur-trading outpost at the confluence of the Mississippi and Wisconsin Rivers. Lockwood condescendingly refers to her as the only person in the region "pretending knowledge of the healing art." But he also praises her midwifery skills and describes her as "an excellent nurse." Her treatment of choice was a "yarb drink" whose ingredients are lost to time.[1]

Even when a formally trained physician arrived in Prairie du Chien, local residents continued to patronize Labuche. Drawing on wisdom passed down from her mother, she gathered roots and plants by the Mississippi and distilled them into healthful tinctures and powders. She treated grateful neighbors in her log house and took her pay in produce. The yarb drink reputedly cured patients when traditional medicine failed. "We frequently joked [with] the physician about Mary Ann's superior skill in the healing art," Lockwood wrote, displaying more than a hint of sexism but also acknowledging Labuche's considerable talent.

In fact, she saved the life of her young granddaughter after a severe head injury. An early twentieth century newspaper account

In Prairie du Chien's Mississippi River Sculpture Park, Marianne Labuche is celebrated as Wisconsin's first doctor. COURTESY OF CJ (MERRIFIELD) PIERSON

reported that she "covered the exposed brain of the infant with a piece of silver, saving its life. The little girl lived 80 years."[2]

Labuche prefigured the women who became doctors in the mid-1800s, such as Laura Ross Wolcott. The third American woman to earn a medical degree, Wolcott launched a practice in Milwaukee in 1856. She endured discrimination in the male medical establishment, which initially rejected her for membership in the Medical Society of Milwaukee County. A report warned that "the Society cannot survive the presence of a woman."[3]

One can imagine the menfolk sneering at the idea of a woman who presumed to be a doctor, just as Lockwood and his physician friend did at the thought of Labuche's ambitions. But, like Labuche, Wolcott and her female colleagues refused to give up the healing arts and transformed the practice of medicine.

Prairie du Chien honors Marianne Labuche's groundbreaking work with a statue in Mississippi River Sculpture Park. She's depicted with her arms wrapped around a baby: the picture of therapeutic care.

Thinkers

89

The Onion

Publication Mocks Major Media Outlets; Becomes One

In the 1970s and '80s, absurdity reigned in Madison's counter-culture. At the University of Wisconsin–Madison, the Pail and Shovel Party constructed a seemingly submerged Statue of Liberty on frozen Lake Mendota. Jim Abrahams and Jerry and David Zucker heckled Hollywood with Kentucky Fried Theater, a precursor to their big-screen farces *Airplane!* and *The Naked Gun*. And in a popular hippie street act, Martin and Loon juggled a Hostess Snowball along with two tomatoes. The jugglers' goal: to take a bite of the nutritious vegetables as they sped by while avoiding an accidental taste of the Snowball, whose overload of chemical additives would presumably lead to instant death.

You couldn't call this goofiness for its own sake. Madison's alienated artists took a satirical stance toward mainstream culture, punking the powers that be.

In such fertile soil, the *Onion* sprouted. UW undergrads Tim Keck and Chris Johnson started the humor publication in 1988 and soon sold it to fellow Madisonians Scott Dikkers and Peter Haise, who envisioned a news parody to end all news parodies. When the weekly paper hit its stride in the 1990s, it told hard truths—at a slant—by mimicking bland *USA Today*–style journalism.

The *Onion* perfected absurdity as a form of hip commentary, using deadpan headlines to deliver extraordinarily trenchant observations.

On corporations run amok: "New Starbucks Opens in Restroom of Existing Starbucks."

On homophobia: "'98 Homosexual-Recruitment Drive Nearing Goal."

On greed: "Nation's Wealthiest One Percent Demands Minority Status."

On media cliches: "Loved Ones Recall Local Man's Cowardly Battle with Cancer."

And on human existence: "World Death Rate Holding Steady at 100 Percent."

Who crafted these one-of-a-kind one-liners, which rank up there with Mark Twain's witticisms and put the era's Ivy League–educated comedy industry to shame? The culprits were familiar Madison types: clerks, dishwashers, UW dropouts, and other outsiders who had always regarded the insiders as ridiculous. Todd Hanson, Carol Kolb, Rob Siegel, John Krewson, Maria Schneider, Ben Karlin, Joe Garden, and company holed up in a cluttered writers' room, generating hundreds of headlines per week and then whittling them down to a handful of concisely worded winners. They worked for love, not money—until the internet helped turn a local phenomenon into an international one.

In 1996, the *Onion*'s new website grabbed the world's attention with an article on the timely subject of foreign intervention: "Clinton Deploys Vowels to Bosnia: Cities of Sjbvdnzv, Grzny to Be First Recipients." That cluttered Madison writers' room soon became the toast of the coasts, with New York City publishing companies, Los Angeles film studios, and would-be corporate investors beating a path to its door. The media outlets the *Onion* loved to mock weighed in with earnest adulation (and groan-inducing headlines like "Peeling *The Onion*") that justified the mockery. The *New Yorker*'s Hendrik Hertzberg superciliously praised the "throwaway" newspaper from the "Corn Belt" in an article filled with ponderous analysis and stuffy jokes. Shortly thereafter, an *Onion* headline demolished the pompous publication with a mere nine words: "Stack of Unread *New Yorkers* Celebrates One-Year Anniversary."

After releasing bestselling books and signing movie deals, the folks behind the *Onion* inevitably moved the operation to New York

City. But that didn't mean selling out; it meant bringing the Madison sensibility to Manhattan.

A few months after the staff arrived in 2001, terrorists bombed the World Trade Center. While other comedians went silent, the *Onion* decided that humor had a role in processing the tragedy. Faced with the near-impossible task of striking the right tone, the writers produced a masterpiece. Headlines from the 9/11 issue gave the country the catharsis it needed by trashing religious extremism: "God Angrily Clarifies 'Don't Kill' Rule." And they showed no mercy to the suicidal bombers who had expected a heavenly reward for their evil act: "Hijackers Surprised to Find Selves in Hell."

The issue was widely praised by major media, and letters poured in from grateful readers who had thought they'd never laugh again. The 9/11 headline that stirred the most emotional response was an uncharacteristically sentimental one, hinting at the heart that had always lurked beneath the *Onion's* humor: "Not Knowing What Else to Do, Woman Bakes American-Flag Cake."

90

Aldo Leopold

Natural, Wild, and Free

I am surrounded by Aldo Leopold. Madison boasts the Aldo Leopold Nature Center, Aldo Leopold Elementary School, Aldo Leopold Park, and Aldo Leopold Memorial Forest. From 1924 to 1948, the University of Wisconsin professor of wildlife management lived in my neighborhood, in a house that's now a Madison landmark. An hour up Highway 12 is a National Historic Landmark, the Sauk County farm where he wrote the conservation bible *A Sand County Almanac*. But for years, despite seeing his name everywhere, I felt no connection to Wisconsin's ecological prophet.

In *A Sand County Almanac*, Leopold famously wrote, "There are some who can live without wild things, and some who cannot." I'm not terribly proud of it, but I can.

Where Aldo grew up fishing, hunting, and exploring the great outdoors in Burlington, Iowa, I came of age on St. Louis concrete. I was violently allergic to the few trees in my environment and relied on allergy shots to prevent sneezing fits. To this day, my usual route—by car—goes from the library to the coffeehouse and back to the library. I feel most comfortable exploring Wisconsin's great indoors.

Thus, I put off reading *A Sand County Almanac*. Whenever Leopold came up at Madison gatherings, I gazed at the floor, shuffled my feet, and excused myself to take a puff from my asthma inhaler.

So imagine my surprise when, late in life, I finally picked up the book and fell in love with it. Now I, too, feel like I can't live without wild things—or at least without reading about them in Leopold's poetic prose.

I admit that I expected stodgy nature writing; instead, I encountered a lively mind at play. Leopold makes himself a character in his essays, and he's charming company during the month-by-month musings on a year at his farm. As he roams his 120 acres or sips coffee by an outdoor fire, you never doubt his affection for everything "natural, wild, and free."[1]

In a typically lyrical passage, he admires the quails at dawn, when "the silence is suddenly broken by a dozen contralto voices, no longer able to restrain their praise of the day to come." You sometimes feel that Leopold, on his solitary wanderings, concocts such stylish phrases just to amuse himself. He anthropomorphizes everything in sight, from fish to birds to skunks and even corn stalks. Rivers are like temperamental painters. Woodcocks are like performers on a stage. "If the chickadee had an office," he writes, "the maxim over his desk would say: 'Keep calm.'"

But Leopold's extravagant conceits have a thematic purpose. If flora and fauna are like humans, we are also like them. That's the theme of *A Sand County Almanac*'s essay on "the land ethic": the connection between humans and everything else on the planet. This philosophy, he says, "changes the role of Homo Sapiens from conqueror of the land-community to plain member and citizen of it. It implies respect for his fellow-members, and also respect for the community as such." You can trace a straight line from this idea to Earth Day, created in 1970 by Wisconsin governor, US senator, and Clear Lake native Gaylord Nelson.

Sadly, Leopold didn't survive to see his work transform our approach to conservation, making *A Sand County Almanac* as influential as Henry David Thoreau's *Walden*. Before publication, he died of a heart attack at age sixty-one while fighting a brush fire near his farm.

You can't help but wonder where his restless thoughts would have taken him if his life had been longer. One of the great pleasures of reading Leopold is seeing his thinking evolve in real time. He admits what he doesn't know and changes his mind in response to experience. The most celebrated example comes in the essay

"Thinking Like a Mountain," in which he describes shooting a wolf, a species he'd considered merely a nuisance for hunters. Approaching the dying creature on a mountain, however, he perceives a "fierce green fire" in her eyes. "I realized then, and have known ever since, that there was something new to me in those eyes— something known only to her and to the mountain," he writes. "I was young then, and full of trigger-itch; I thought that because fewer wolves meant more deer, that no wolves would mean hunters' paradise. But after seeing the green fire die, I sensed that neither the wolf nor the mountain agreed."

Such affecting passages have convinced me to start thinking more like a mountain myself. And I might even try doing it outdoors.

91

Harriet Bell Merrill

Hunting for the Unseen

I never had a limnologist hero until I learned of Harriet Bell Merrill, who advanced the field while gleefully ignoring restrictions for women in the early twentieth century. Wearing a pair of men's high-top boots, she traveled solo through South America to conduct research for the University of Wisconsin and collect samples for the Milwaukee Public Museum. Her brother insisted that it was "entirely out of the question for a petite little woman to hazard such a rigorous venture."[1] Yet Merrill made a career of doing things that were entirely out of the question for women.

Born in Stevens Point in 1863, she grew up fascinated by the Wisconsin River. Rather than fitting into a conventional role, the budding scientist collected rocks, insects, and plants to scrutinize under a microscope. She graduated summa cum laude from the UW in 1890 at a time when many disapproved of women students. Eyebrows rose when she hiked up her skirts to collect specimens in muddy fields and lakes, a bulky camera around her neck.

In Milwaukee, Merrill taught science to high school and college students. She earned a master's degree at the University of Chicago and joined the UW faculty as a pioneering female professor of zoology, specializing in water fleas. In 1902, she realized her lifelong dream: conducting fieldwork in South America. Shrugging off the naysayers, Merrill laced up her men's boots and boarded the SS *Byron* in New York City. She considered it "a release as liberating as loosening the constraints of corset stays and changing to a shift."[2]

From the get-go, the journey tested her mettle. On board, cockroaches swarmed her pillow and found their way into her teacup.

During a 1902 trek through South America, fearless scientist
Harriet Bell Merrill braved wild animals and perilous rivers.
COURTESY OF LYNN CASPER

And on the two-thousand-mile trek through remote parts of Brazil,
Paraguay, and Argentina, she braved wild animals and perilous rivers.
Merrill carried on despite the threat of cholera, yellow fever, and
bubonic plague. On one hike, her boots sank into the mud with every
step while six-inch thorns shredded her clothes. By the time she
reached a clearing, she wrote in her notebook, "I felt I had awakened
from a nightmare."[3]

But the notebook also captures Merrill's sense of wonder as she
collected plant and animal specimens, many of them new to scientists. "Enormous tropical butterflies cluster together like fluttering
masses of bright blossoms," she wrote, "all open to the heavens
where colorful species of birds and insects fly unwarily about in a
symbiotic paradise."[4]

As a woman traveling mostly alone, Merrill entered local legend. South American newspapers printed flowery accounts of her exploits, though writers seemed perplexed by her footwear. They dubbed her "the courageous American woman."[5]

At the end of her expedition, Merrill had reason to be proud. "I believe, when I left home, that many of my friends thought I would never return alive," she stated, "but they were mistaken."[6] She examined the more than seven hundred samples she'd collected, published articles about her trip in the *Milwaukee Sentinel*, and presented her findings at the University of Chicago and Cornell University.

Despite ill health, Merrill made another arduous trek through South America and the Caribbean five years later, visiting Brazil, Venezuela, Trinidad, British Guiana, and Curaçao. "I keep hunting for the 'unseen' through the rain forests and waterways," she wrote.[7]

In 1915, the fearless scientist died from a heart condition at age fifty-two while pursuing her PhD at the University of Illinois. The world virtually forgot about her until the 1990s, when her grandniece Merrilyn Hartridge published a biography. I hope future generations remember Harriet Bell Merrill for excelling in a male-dominated field when few thought she could.

Happily, the surname "Merrill" is guaranteed to live on forever in the annals of science. One of her fellow UW researchers named a species of crustacean in her honor: *Diaptomus Merrilli*.

92

Ann Landers and Abigail Van Buren

A Sweetheart of a Time in Eau Claire

Ann Landers and Abigail Van Buren were advice-column royalty from the 1950s into the twenty-first century. *Dear Abby* once reigned as the world's most popular newspaper column, with 110 million readers. *Ask Ann Landers* came right behind with 90 million. Before then, Ann and Abby—a.k.a. twin sisters Esther and Pauline Friedman—spent a decade as stay-at-home moms in Eau Claire, with no inkling of the fame and fortune to come.

Esther and Pauline were born to Russian Jewish immigrants in Sioux City, Iowa, and they grew up doing everything in tandem. They sang Andrews Sisters duets in Yiddish, wore matching raccoon coats, and collaborated on a college gossip column. Naturally, they also had a double wedding in identical dresses and veils, becoming Esther Lederer and Pauline Phillips.

In the 1940s, the twins moved to Eau Claire, where both husbands had jobs at the National Presto appliance company. Esther and Pauline cut glamorous figures in their new town. They dined at Austin's White House supper club, hosted elaborate soirees, and led parades in a Cadillac convertible. They also became fixtures at Eau Claire Bears baseball games, turning heads at Carson Park in their lacquered hairstyles.

The sisters didn't just party in Eau Claire; they also pitched in for the community. They cultivated their listening skills and empathy by volunteering for the Red Cross. Esther served as chair of the county's Democratic Party, denouncing Wisconsin demagogue Joseph McCarthy. "Our days in Eau Claire shall be savored with nostalgic and loving recollections," Pauline later wrote. "What a sweetheart of a time we had in that small Wisconsin town!"[1]

In the mid-1950s, the twins finally separated—Esther moving to Chicago and Pauline to San Francisco—but they continued on the same track. Esther read the antiquated advice column in the *Chicago Sun-Times* and thought, "Not great." Pauline read the one in the *San Francisco Chronicle* and thought, "I can do better." Each brashly submitted sample columns and won over their respective editors, with Esther assuming the pseudonym Ann Landers and Pauline dubbing herself Abigail Van Buren. The advice biz would never be the same.

The columns had distinct styles: *Ask Ann Landers* dished out detailed responses, while *Dear Abby* favored one-line quips. But both women brought a merciless wit and up-to-date directness to the prim-and-proper genre. They took on touchy subjects and pulled no punches with their relatively liberal opinions. Esther and Pauline did their research, quoted experts, and evolved with the times (thank goodness!) on cultural issues like divorce and homophobia. As in their Red Cross days in Eau Claire, they were motivated by a desire to help people. Pauline was even known to telephone readers who'd written in with suicidal thoughts.

While the women solved other people's problems, they had a harder time with one of their own: advice-column rivalry. Each developed a set of grievances, and their conflict went painfully public. With only slight exaggeration, a 1958 article in *Life* magazine called it "the most feverish female feud since Elizabeth sent Mary Queen of Scots to the chopping block."[2] The two reconciled in 1964, but hard feelings remained. In a 1979 TV appearance, Esther revealed that she never read *Dear Abby*. In a magazine interview two years later, Pauline called Esther envious and inferior.

You have to wonder if, at the end of their lives, the siblings pined for the innocent pleasures of Eau Claire, that "small Wisconsin town" where they had "a sweetheart of a time." Both had become wildly successful since then, named in polls as the country's most influential women. But if given the chance, who knows? They may well have traded in their professional resentments to be back in Carson Park, arm in arm, blissfully cheering on the Eau Claire Bears.

93

Esther Lederberg

Credit Where Credit's Due

When husband-and-wife scientists Joshua and Esther Lederberg posed for a photo at the 1958 Nobel Prize ceremony, just one of them looked happy. Facing the flashbulbs in a tuxedo, Joshua smiled. And why not? The Nobel committee had immortalized him and his two male colleagues for their work in microbial genetics.

At his side, in a gown and elbow-length gloves, Esther did not smile. Indeed, her stony stare could have melted the camera. She had received no share of the Nobel, despite her key contributions. And Joshua scarcely acknowledged her in his remarks.

So let's acknowledge her here.

Born in 1922, Esther Zimmer entered a world that undervalued female scientists. At Hunter College in the late 1930s, she studied biochemistry despite teachers who told her the subject was too hard for women. She continued defying the naysayers and earned a master's degree in genetics at Stanford University, where she met the scientist who would become her first husband, Joshua Lederberg. After the couple moved to the University of Wisconsin in the late 1940s, Esther received her PhD, joined her husband's lab, and contributed to a revolution in the field of microbiology.

Esther's male colleagues hailed her creativity with a pipette and a petri dish. Working from her UW lab bench, she made major breakthroughs that revealed how microorganisms share genetic material. She discovered the lambda bacteriophage, a parasite that became a model for studying viruses and genetics, setting the stage for understanding DNA. She discovered the bacterial fertility factor called the F-plasmid. And she helped develop a transformative technique called replica plating, which allowed geneticists to dupli-cate bacterial colonies using sterilized scraps of velvet. Nothing if not resourceful, Esther initially tested the method with the powder puff from her makeup kit.

The husband-and-wife team published papers together and shared the 1956 Pasteur Award for contributions to science. Never-theless, Joshua regularly received sole credit for work they did together. Fast forward to her stony stare at the Nobel ceremony.

Esther's colleague Stanley Falkow later stated that Esther's "independent seminal contributions in Joshua's laboratory . . . surely led, in part, to his Nobel Prize."[1] Lise Meitner, who helped discover nuclear fission in 1938; Chien-Shiung Wu, who made an essential particle and nuclear physics discovery in 1956; and other women scientists passed over for Nobels must have known how she felt.

After a decade in Madison, the couple returned to Stanford, where Joshua was treated like royalty while Esther was offered an untenured position with scant funding to continue her research. And thus did a brilliant female scientist pass into obscurity. "If Esther would have been a man," said her biographer Rebecca Ferrell, "all kinds of things would have been different."[2]

Joshua developed big-ego syndrome following the Nobel Prize, and the couple divorced in 1966. Esther spent the next part of her life advocating for women, pursuing her passion for literature and music, and founding Stanford's Plasmid Reference Center. She died in 2006, certain that she'd be forgotten.

Luckily, it didn't happen, thanks to advocacy by Esther's second husband and various writers and scientists. Now you, too, can spread the word and keep her memory alive.

94

Will Allen

Growing Power

If you happened to drive through Milwaukee's north side in the early 2000s, you might have been surprised to encounter—among the fast-food joints, convenience stores, and vacant lots—a farm. One with chickens and goats, fruits and vegetables, and Black, white, Hmong, and Latino farmers working together in fragrant greenhouses.

The Growing Power farm was an unlikely Garden of Eden, powered by sunshine, organic fertilizer, and dreams. Will Allen, who conjured it out of inner-city concrete, labored to spread his vision of healthy food throughout Milwaukee, then Wisconsin, then the world. His goal was nothing less than healing humanity in body and spirit via sustainable agriculture. And it all grew out of five broken-down greenhouses on West Silver Spring Street.

Allen is a descendant of African American farmers who struggled under the depredations of slavery and sharecropping. After a stint as a college and pro basketball player—during which a Florida journalist described him as "a snorting terror of rippling muscle"—he moved to Oak Creek to work in the corporate world and pursue his true passion, farming, on the side.[1] On the way to a business appointment in 1993, he spotted a for-sale sign on the last parcel of land in Milwaukee zoned for agricultural use. Given to thinking big, he saw beyond the greenhouses' cracked glass panes and imagined an operation that could nourish an impoverished community with a healthy alternative to Popeye's and McDonald's.

Allen built a nonprofit organization through trial and error, brainstorm by brainstorm, defying the odds for a small farmer.

By 2011, Will Allen had turned his farm into an urban Garden of Eden, spreading the gospel of a "good food revolution." PHOTO BY PETE AMLAND (UWM PHOTOGRAPHIC SERVICES), CC-BY-2.0

Hemmed in by his two-acre lot, he expanded vertically with multiple tiers of spinach and arugula. He devised ingenious systems for cultivating fish, sprouts, honey, and compost. Most impressive, he forged bonds with local people and businesses to create a multipronged community effort that provided classes, youth projects, and school lunches. Before long, Allen was employing scores of neighbors and providing forty tons of fresh produce a year to those who would otherwise have trouble affording it.

Word got out about the miracle on West Silver Spring Street. Allen received glowing press, major foundation support, and a MacArthur Fellowship "genius grant." In 2010, *Time* magazine included him on its annual list of remarkable people, in such company as Steve Jobs, Oprah Winfrey, and Serena Williams. He began exporting his "good food revolution" (per the title of his 2012 book) to underserved communities around the country with workshops, conferences, and training centers. Ten thousand visitors a year from around the world tramped through the Growing Power facility to witness urban ecology in action.

"When you're growing sustainably, and not using chemicals, you have your ups and downs," Allen acknowledged as he neared age seventy.[2] Growing Power went down for the count in 2017 after a twenty-four-year run, but that was hardly the end of its story. Many of its workers graduated to their own urban-farming operations, including Allen's daughter, Erika, who went on to become a food activist in Chicago. And many people inspired by Growing Power transformed their own neighborhoods. Ricardo Salvador, director of the food and environment program at the Union of Concerned Scientists, said, "The training, learning, and benefits of Growing Power will be felt for years to come."[3]

That, of course, is what happens when you plant a seed.

95

Mike Wilmington

For the Love of Movies

When I was an editor at the Madison newsweekly *Isthmus*, I could count on an immediate phone call from freelance movie critic Mike Wilmington whenever a significant film personality died. Mike—invariably broken up by the news—would beg to write a tribute. Could we clear out space in the next issue for, say, three thousand words?

I had mixed feelings about these calls. On the one hand, no, I didn't want to rearrange the entire issue at the last minute. On the other hand, I knew Mike would write an essay to end all essays— and for the pittance *Isthmus* paid freelancers. It didn't matter that he no longer lived in Madison or that he already had plenty to do as a nationally renowned movie critic for the *Los Angeles Times* and later the *Chicago Tribune*. He wanted—he *needed*—to write this piece for Madison readers. For the publication and the city he still loved.

So I'd rearrange the entire issue at the last minute. And we would run the fervent tribute to Orson Welles, or François Truffaut, or Warren Oates, to readers' delight.

Wilmington had a hardscrabble childhood in Williams Bay, then immersed himself in the 1960s Madison counterculture, hot for changing the world. As an undergrad at the University of Wisconsin, he marched against the Vietnam War and appeared onstage in 1968's notorious theatrical adaptation of *Peter Pan*, an anti-establishment parable in the nude. His UW gang—which included other obsessive cinephiles like Joseph McBride, who would later become his collaborator on a book about director John Ford—went on to achieve fame in Hollywood circles as "The Madison Mafia."

As an erudite young film critic for the UW's *Daily Cardinal* in the late 1960s and '70s, and then for *Isthmus* starting in the early '80s, Wilmington worshiped a personal pantheon of filmmakers like Welles, Ford, and Alfred Hitchcock, who in his estimation could do no wrong. Indeed, he felt deeply wounded when others disparaged their work. He made it his life's mission to exalt them wherever and whenever he could.

That's why, when he moved to Los Angeles in the 1980s for a movie critic job at the *LA Weekly*, he tried to singlehandedly revive the public's interest in Welles. It's why he insisted on covering every Hitchcock rerelease for *Isthmus*, including a review of *Rope*—a film seemingly shot in one continuous take—that paid tribute to the director's formal inventiveness with a single, labyrinthine, five-hundred-word sentence.

When writing of his cinematic heroes, Wilmington grasped for ever-greater superlatives, like an operatic tenor reaching for higher and higher notes. I remember one urgent call before press time when he insisted that I change a descriptor in his review from "scintillating" to "coruscating"—because, on second thought, "scintillating" just didn't have the proper intensity.

Wilmington died in 2022, and my favorite memory of him is, fittingly, set in a Madison movie theater. He'd returned to town to speak at a film festival, and I attended a screening with him for the first and only time. I often had trouble connecting the dour character I knew from our long-distance phone calls with the giddy enthusiast I encountered in his writing. Sitting next to Mike in the theater, however, I saw up close what movies could do to him. With his face bathed in light from the silver screen, he seemed transfigured by joy.

If there's a heaven, Mike Wilmington is probably sitting in some otherworldly movie theater right now—his own version of eternal bliss.

96

Sigurd Olson

Cosmic Purpose

Sigurd Olson embodies the Up-North folk hero. He explored the wilderness with a philosophical perspective, toiling over lyrical essays at his desk while also jumping at every opportunity for adventure on a trail or a lake. Americans revere him as an environmental activist who never gave up the fight, even when pro-development forces hanged him in effigy.

You might assume that Olson emerged from northern timber, like Paul Bunyan, with a fishing rod in one hand, a compass in the other, and snowshoes on his feet. In fact, he came from gritty Chicago, the son of a strict Baptist minister with little interest in the outdoors. It wasn't until his family moved to Wisconsin that seven-year-old Sigurd found his true love.

In Sister Bay, the boy took his first steps away from his oppressive home life and into the unknown. One fateful day, he wandered through the woods and came upon majestic Lake Michigan. As the waves crashed and the seagulls cawed, he remembered, "I was alone in a wild and lovely place, part of the dark forest through which I had come, and of all the wild sounds and colors and feelings of the place I had found." That day, Olson testified, he "entered into a life of indescribable beauty and delight."[1]

The adventure continued when his family moved farther north to Prentice, on the rocky Jump River. Sigurd learned to hunt with a slingshot and catch trout with a sewing-thread line. The family's next home was the harbor town of Ashland, where he began his romance with Lake Superior. He canoed in Chequamegon Bay and tramped across the Apostle Islands, seeing in nature what he called a cosmic purpose. In a sign of things to come, he won an Ashland high school writing contest.

Anyone might have guessed what Olson was born to do—anyone but Olson. Under his father's baleful influence, he studied agriculture and geology at Ashland's Northland College and the University of Wisconsin in Madison, with the idea of becoming a teacher and a missionary. He did work in higher education for a time, but then a revelatory canoe trip in northern Minnesota set him on a different path. Like his predecessor (and Montello resident) John Muir, Olson would spend the rest of his life traversing the wilderness, reflecting on it, and doing his damnedest to protect it.

The Singing Wilderness (1956), *Listening Point* (1958), and *Reflections from the North Country* (1976) became nature-writing classics. Olson's activism, which included a strenuous effort to preserve the Boundary Waters Canoe Area Wilderness near his home base of Ely, Minnesota, eventually earned him a spot in the National Wildlife Federation's Conservation Hall of Fame. "By saving any wilderness," Olson said, "what you are really saving is the human spirit."[2]

In 1971, Northland College honored its famous alumnus by launching the Sigurd Olson Environmental Institute, which addresses environmental challenges in his beloved Lake Superior region. To this day, you can view his snowshoes and other prized possessions in the institute's display case.

Olson liked nothing better than snowshoeing around his favorite bog in Ely. He died in that bog in 1982, leaving an unfinished piece in his typewriter back home. The last words he typed stand as an epitaph: "A new adventure is coming up and I know it will be a good one."[3]

97

Har Gobind Khorana

Cracking the Genetic Code

University of Wisconsin scientist Har Gobind Khorana won the 1968 Nobel Prize for his transformative work on the genetic code. Pretty impressive for a man whose education began not in a school, but under a tree.

Khorana's impoverished family lived in the tiny Indian village of Raipur in a home that doubled as a stable, with bedrooms at one end and horses and cows at the other. Young Gobind had to steal sugarcane from nearby fields and collect embers from neighbors' fires to use for cooking. The village had no school, so he learned to read and write under that tree with his father as tutor. Pencils were a scarce commodity, and Gobind cherished them. For the rest of his life, he refused to part with one until it had been whittled down to a nub.

After four years of studying under the tree, Gobind attended a one-room school that his father helped establish in the village. By the time he was a teenager, his intellectual gifts were evident and led to a scholarship offer from Punjab University. Gobind was too shy to attend the mandatory admissions interview, but no matter. The school accepted him anyway in a rare triumph of good sense over senseless bureaucracy. The young man rode out of Raipur on an elephant to meet his destiny—which he thought was English literature.

Luckily, the university's entrance exam for English classes included an oral component, and once again Khorana's shyness got the better of him. He didn't take the exam and opted for chemistry as a second choice, beginning a scientific journey that would change the world.

Har Gobind Khorana, pictured with a model of a synthesized gene circa 1970, won a Nobel Prize for finding solutions to seemingly unsolvable problems.
UNIVERSITY OF WISCONSIN-MADISON ARCHIVES

After receiving his bachelor's and master's degrees at Punjab in the 1940s, Khorana attended a series of universities and subsisted on rice and milk while delving into the mysteries of DNA and RNA. Colleagues noted his combination of childlike enthusiasm, intense drive, and attention to detail. He had a penchant for tackling seemingly unsolvable problems and then chipping away until he solved them.

When Khorana arrived at the University of Wisconsin in 1960 to direct the Institute for Enzyme Research, the problem was the genetic code. As the head of a multidisciplinary team—an unusual approach for the time—he sought to understand how genetic instructions control the way a cell produces proteins. Members of his lab worked around the clock in double shifts, with success following success. Their breakthroughs revolutionized our understanding of genes, created new ways of combating illness, and earned Khorana the title of "the father of chemical biology."[1]

They also earned him the Nobel Prize, though he wasn't the type to bask in glory. Indeed, he was one of the last people to learn he'd won the award. While a less humble scientist might have sat by the phone, waiting for a call from Stockholm, Gobind was holed up in a rented cottage outside of Madison with no connection to the outside world. His wife, Esther, had to drive over to deliver the news.

Khorana was using his time in the cottage to work on another paper. As usual, he remained focused on solving the next seemingly unsolvable problem.

98

Adda Howie

Concerts for Cows

In the late nineteenth and early twentieth centuries, Wisconsin's progressive movement had a powerful influence on national politics, leading to improved workplace conditions, cleaner government, and curbs on big business. It also led to mandolin music for cows.

The latter reform came courtesy of Adda Howie, who achieved fame as the United States' "most successful woman farmer."[1] Farming had long been dominated by men, but Howie devised new techniques—including lace curtains on barn windows—that transformed agricultural practices around the world.

Adda Johnston grew up on Sunny Peak Farm in Brookfield Township, sharing an idyllic girlhood with her sister. She left rural life when she married wealthy industrialist David Howie and settled into a fashionable Milwaukee neighborhood. But in a twist of fate, she inherited Sunny Peak Farm in 1897, at age forty-five. What would an urban socialite do with 120 acres, two cows, and several rundown outbuildings?

As a good progressive, Howie turned to science, the movement's cure-all for any social ill. She dispatched her son to take agriculture courses in Madison and applied herself to studying the history of cattle. The family moved back to the Brookfield village of Elm Grove, where Howie embarked on a modernization drive. Channeling the ambition of her can-do era, she aimed to create a farming system that others could emulate. And at a time when women were marching for suffrage, she made no apologies for what she considered feminine values, with an emphasis on nurturing, aesthetics, and cleanliness.

Adda Howie, pictured on Sunny Peak Farm around 1909, viewed
livestock not merely as units of production, but as good company.
WHI IMAGE ID 129425

Howie would not trample everything in her path for the sake of
profit, as did the hated monopolies. Instead, she treated her assets
with care, including the cows. She played her mandolin for them
and sang "In the Gloaming," a herd favorite. Her method assumed
that lovingly tended livestock would be more productive—and
laugh all you want, but Howie's cows set records, quintupling the
yields of their less-coddled peers.

The curtains she put up in the barn not only looked charming
but also kept away the flies. She scrubbed the outbuildings with
soap and boiling water and required milkers to wash their hands
in order to prevent disease. Such innovations brought prosperity,
and she soon possessed Wisconsin's largest herd of purebred Jersey cows.

The world took notice. European magazines reprinted images
of her joyous cattle concerts. International conferences clamored
for speaking appearances. Japan sent an emissary to Elm Grove
to buy some of Howie's cows, hoping for an instant uptick in the
nation's dairy stock. An Arizona newspaper called her "one of the

most famous women in the United States—one about whom more has been written and printed in this and foreign countries than about any other woman now living."[2]

Indeed, her fame has persisted decades after her death in 1936. In 2020, Darlington's Lucky Cow gelato shop unveiled a flavor called "Lady Howie"—created, presumably, with milk from well-loved cows.

In an age that had little interest in the humane treatment of animals, Howie emerged as a beacon of enlightened thought. She viewed livestock not merely as units of production, but as good company. As she once said, "Cows make the best of friends."[3]

99

Margaret H'Doubler

Connecting Mind and Body

In the 1920s, Wisconsin had an international reputation for making cheese, brewing beer, and—believe it or not—training dancers. It rivaled New York as a dance capital, and all because of one idealistic woman, Margaret H'Doubler, who put her heart and soul into establishing the country's first dance major at the University of Wisconsin. For H'Doubler, dance involved more than mastering leaps and lunges. It meant helping people reach their full potential as creative beings.

To our ears, dance as a means of self-expression sounds self-evident. But that's in large part because H'Doubler energetically advanced the idea during the early twentieth century—a more puritanical era, when most folks were not in the habit of freely moving their bodies. As H'Doubler spread the gospel of dance as a physical, emotional, and intellectual pursuit, UW president Edward Birge feared the increasing popularity of her methods. "We can't have the university known as a dancing school," he warned her.[1]

Margaret had been an adventurous child, unwilling to accept the limitations imposed on women around the turn of the century. She attended high school in Madison and played basketball and field hockey. At the University of Wisconsin, she majored in biology but also worked out with wands and barbells in the gymnasium. After graduation, the UW hired her in its newly established Department of Physical Education for Women, where her warmth and enthusiasm attracted hordes of students.

H'Doubler's search for new ways of connecting mind and body led her to a workshop in New York City where children learned

Margaret H'Doubler, pictured in 1972, pioneered the idea of dance as self-expression. UNIVERSITY OF WISCONSIN-MADISON ARCHIVES

about movement while lying on the floor. This was her eureka moment. "Of course," she thought. "Get on the floor where the pull of gravity is relieved and see how the body will react. Study the body's structure and its response."[2]

With heart aflame, H'Doubler returned to Madison and launched the first dance classes at a US university. She did indeed put students on the floor—lying down, crawling, wearing blindfolds—to release them from their inhibitions and to reacquaint them with their own bodies. With her background in biology, she employed a skeleton to educate them about bones, joints, and muscles, providing a scientific foundation for their explorations of movement. Orchesis, the troupe she formed for undergrads in 1918, demonstrated the H'Doubler approach to dance on its influential college tours.

The academic world hardly knew what to make of all this. Despite President Birge's best efforts, the University of Wisconsin had, indeed, become known as a dancing school.

In 1926, H'Doubler created the nation's first dance major and gave the art form a scholarly cachet that persists to this day. She published books based on her classes and took her place among modern-dance pioneers Martha Graham and Doris Humphrey. UW grads disseminated her ideas as they joined prominent dance troupes and university faculties. Two famous acolytes, Mary Hinkson and Anna Halprin, performed phenomenal feats on stage because H'Doubler had convinced them that they could.

"She made people feel they were very special," a UW colleague once said. "That was her real philosophy."[3]

100

Chia Youyee Vang

Collector of Stories

Can a collector of other people's stories be a hero? I'm biased myself (see: the book you're currently reading), but my pantheon retains a special place for folklorists, biographers, and oral historians who venture down roads less traveled to document lives for future generations. Famously, Zora Neale Hurston preserved African American folk tales from her native Florida, and William Herndon gathered revelatory accounts of Abraham Lincoln after the president's assassination. In Wisconsin, Chia Youyee Vang has made it her mission to chronicle the Hmong people who settled in the United States following the Vietnam War—a community close to her heart.

Vang grew up in Laos, where the United States government secretly recruited fighters, her father among them, to help defeat regional communists in the 1960s and '70s. When the communists prevailed, her family fled for their lives, racing through jungles in the middle of the night. They joined thousands of other Hmong in a refugee camp in Thailand, then moved to the United States. But relocation didn't solve all their problems.

At eight years old, Vang faced daunting challenges in her new home of St. Paul, Minnesota: poverty, racism, bullying. She escaped by immersing herself in books, such as the Little House series by Pepin-born author Laura Ingalls Wilder. Education became her salvation, and ultimately her career.

Vang earned a doctorate in American studies and took her work in an innovative direction. She began studying her own Hmong American community as a researcher and history professor at the

University of Wisconsin–Milwaukee, where she founded a Hmong Diaspora Studies program. Her interviews with veterans who'd been swept up in the United States' covert war yielded her first publication, *Fly Until You Die: An Oral History of Hmong Pilots in the Vietnam War*. Another book, *Hmong America: Reconstructing Community in Diaspora*, explores Hmong refugees' efforts to gain a foothold in the United States, including a significant settlement in Wisconsin. Vang interviews sources and shows up at events, making an intimate connection with her subjects. "When language is not a barrier between researcher and interviewee," she writes in *Hmong America*, "I believe that stories are told and experiences are explained differently due to the existence of a common cultural knowledge."[1]

Vang gravitates toward ordinary people, believing their lives are just as significant as those of leaders and celebrities. In *Hmong America*, for example, she explores the spiritual journeys of Xao Vue, who moved to Sheboygan in 1982, and her mother-in-law, Shoua Vue. Xao's child healed after a pastor prayed for them at the local Christian church; that was enough to make her a believer. Shoua, a shaman, had a similar conversion experience. She fell gravely ill but then recovered in the hospital. "I could see angels in white uniforms coming down to tell me that I would be saved if I believed," Vang quotes her as saying. "When we came home, I threw away all of my shaman equipments and never looked back."

Hmong Americans like the Vues are enriching American life, just as refugees from other countries did before them. When the first and second generations pass from living memory, people will wonder how it felt for them to leave Laos, arrive in the United States, and maintain cultural traditions while assimilating to new surroundings.

Thanks to Vang, there will be no shortage of stories.

Acknowledgments

My wife, Ann, and child, Jo, are brilliant writers who helped me dream *Wisconsin Idols* into existence. Credit to Jo for the initial good idea and to Ann for innumerable other good ideas as the book came together.

My thanks to Kate Thompson for kindly bringing this project to the Wisconsin Historical Society Press; copyeditor Melissa York for her sharp eye; and agent extraordinaire Marietta Zacker for invaluable assistance. Editor Elizabeth Wyckoff helped shape the manuscript with consummate skill, from the grand conception to the smallest detail. She has been a true partner.

Several of the book's chapters originally appeared elsewhere, in different form, benefiting from the editorial insights of John Allen, Judith Davidoff, Niki Denison, Erika Janik, Maureen McCollum, Bruce Murphy, Megan Provost, Preston Schmitt, and Anne Strainchamps.

The chapters on Roscoe Mitchell and Mike Wilmington were originally published in *Isthmus*. The chapters on Avi, Zona Gale, and Michael Mann were originally published in *On Wisconsin*. And the following chapters were originally broadcast on Wisconsin Public Radio's Wisconsin Life: Hank Aaron; the Beatles; Bunny Berigan; Edward Berner, George Hallauer, and the Girl from Two Rivers; the Chordettes; Laurel Clark; Richard Davis; Duke Ellington; Chris Farley; Harrison Ford; Grafton Blues Musicians; Woody Herman; Buddy Holly; Harry Houdini; Ann Landers and Abigail Van Buren; Liberace; Abraham Lincoln; Allen Ludden; Fred Merkle; Joni Mitchell; Frank Morgan; Nirvana and Butch Vig; Georgia O'Keeffe; Les Paul; Elvis Presley; Meinhardt Raabe; the

Racine Belles and Kenosha Comets; Otis Redding; Jackie Robinson; Viola Smith; Orson Welles; Oprah Winfrey; and Frank Lloyd Wright and Pedro Guerrero.

Resources

The Chordettes
Slotnick, Daniel E. "Lynn Evans Mand, 95, Dies; a Voice on 'Mr. Sandman' and 'Lollipop.'" *New York Times*, February 28, 2020.

Nirvana and Butch Vig
Cross, Charles. *Heavier Than Heaven: A Biography of Kurt Cobain*. New York: Hachette Books, 2019.

Liberace
Liberace. *The Legendary Liberace* (MPI Home Video DVD, 2002).

Buddy Holly
Norman, Philip. *Rave On: The Biography of Buddy Holly*. New York: Simon & Schuster, 1996.

Otis Redding
Gould, Jonathan. *Otis Redding: An Unfinished Life*. New York: Crown Archetype, 2017.

Viola Smith
Robbins, Dean. *The Fastest Drummer*. Somerville, MA: Candlewick, 2024.
Tucker, Sherrie. *Swing Shift: "All Girl" Bands of the 1940s*. Durham, North Carolina: Duke University Press, 2000.

Grafton Blues Musicians
Palmer, Robert. *Deep Blues: A Musical and Cultural History of the Mississippi Delta*. New York: Penguin Books, 1982.

Little Richard
Cortés, Lisa, dir. *Little Richard: I Am Everything*. Magnolia Home Entertainment, 2023. DVD.

Lynda Barry
Gavaler, Chris. "How to Draw Like a Child and Become a Better Person: Lynda Barry's *Making Comics*." *Pop Matters*, October 28, 2019. www.popmatters.com/lynda-barry-making-comics-2641124780.html.

Dickey Chapelle
Chapelle, Dickey. *What's a Woman Doing Here?: A Reporter's Report on Herself*. New York: Morrow, 1962.
Garofolo, John. *Dickey Chapelle Under Fire: Photographs by the First American Female War Correspondent Killed in Action*. Madison: Wisconsin Historical Society Press, 2015.

Georgia O'Keeffe

Lisle, Laurie. *Portrait of an Artist: A Biography of Georgia O'Keeffe.* Albuquerque: University of New Mexico Press, 1986.

Frank Lloyd Wright and Pedro Guerrero

Guerrero, Pedro E. *A Photographer's Journey.* New York: Princeton Architectural Press, 2007.

———. *Picturing Wright: An Album from Frank Lloyd Wright's Photographer.* San Francisco: Pomegranate Artbooks, 1994.

Helen Farnsworth Mears

Wisconsin Department of Administration, Division of State Facilities. East Wing Architects, LLC. *Historic Structure Report: Wisconsin State Capitol, Book I: Comprehensive Volume.* State of Wisconsin Collection, November 2004.

H. H. Bennett

Bamberger, Tom. *H. H. Bennett: A Sense of Place.* Milwaukee, WI: Milwaukee Art Museum, 1992.

Rath, Sara. *Pioneer Photographer, Wisconsin's H. H. Bennett.* Madison, WI: Tamarack Press, 1979.

Temmer, Jim. "A Compelling Vision: H. H. Bennett and the Wisconsin Dells." *Wisconsin Magazine of History* 85, no. 4 (Summer 2002): 12–19.

Chris Farley

Farley, Tom. *The Chris Farley Show: A Biography in Three Acts.* New York: Viking, 2008.

Harrison Ford

Targo, Steve. "What Do Harrison Ford and Paul Newman Have in Common? Belfry Theatre." *Lake Geneva News*, December 28, 2020.

Gena Rowlands

Feinberg, Scott. "Gena Rowlands: 'I Never Wanted to Be Anything but an Actress.'" *The Hollywood Reporter*, January 10, 2015.

Harry Houdini

Gresham, William Lindsay. *Houdini: The Man Who Walked through Walls.* New York: Holt, 1959.

Carrie Coon

Price, Jenny. "The Accidental Actor." *On Wisconsin*, Summer 2013.

Spencer Tracy

"Spencer Tracy's Early Acting Career Started in Ripon." *Ripon Commonwealth Press*, June 9, 2022. www.riponpress.com/news/throwback -thursday-spencer-tracy-s-early-acting-career-started-in-ripon/article _def23ede-e6a5-11ec-ac49-93261982e028.html.

Mary Hinkson
Long, Harvey. "Dance, Dance Revolutionary." *On Wisconsin*, Summer 2019.

Uta Hagen
Hagen, Uta. *A Challenge for the Actor*. New York: Scribner's, 1991.

Eric and Beth Heiden
"Good as Gold: U.S. Dazzlers Eric and Beth Heiden." *Time*, February 11, 1980.

Fred Merkle
"Fred Merkle, 67, Ball Player, Dies; Giant 1st Baseman 'Boner' in Failing to Touch 2nd Led to Loss of '08 Pennant." *New York Times*, March 3, 1956.

Mildred Fish-Harnack
Donner, Rebecca. *All the Frequent Troubles of Our Days: The True Story of the American Woman at the Heart of the German Resistance to Hitler*. New York: Little, Brown and Company, 2021.

Abraham Lincoln
Donald, David Herbert. *Lincoln*. New York: Simon & Schuster, 1995.

Kathryn Clarenbach
Clarenbach, Kathryn. UW–Madison Oral History Program interview, 1987–89. https://ohms.library.wisc.edu/viewer.php?cachefile=-Clarenbach.K.466-1.xml.
Price, Jenny. "This Woman's Work." *On Wisconsin*, Fall 2016.

Ada James
Bower, Jerry L. "A Biographical Sketch of Ada James." Richland County Historical Society, April 2013. https://richlandcountyhistorical society.weebly.com/uploads/1/2/8/7/12872640/ada_james_april _2013.pdf.

Jesus Salas
Salas, Jesus. *Obreros Unidos: The Roots and Legacy of the Farmworkers Movement*. Madison: Wisconsin Historical Society Press, 2023.

Marianne Labuche
Antoine, Mary Elise. *Enslaved, Indentured, Free: Five Black Women on the Upper Mississippi, 1800–1850*. Madison: Wisconsin Historical Society Press, 2022.

The Onion
Dikkers, Scott, ed., and Robert Siegel and Mike Loew. *The Onion's Finest News Reporting, Volume One*. New York: Three Rivers Press, 2000.
Hertzberg, Hendrik. "Humor Paper Read, Praised." *The New Yorker*, May 10, 1999.

Ann Landers and Abigail Van Buren
Howard, Margo. *Eppie: The Story of Ann Landers*. New York: Putnam, 1982.

Esther Lederberg
Esther M. Zimmer Lederberg Memorial Website, www.estherlederberg .com/.
Schindler, Thomas E. *A Hidden Legacy: The Life and Work of Esther Zimmer Lederberg*. New York: Oxford University Press, 2021.

Will Allen
Allen, Will, with Charles Wilson. *The Good Food Revolution: Growing Healthy Food, People, and Communities*. New York: Gotham Books, 2012.

Har Gobind Khorana
Mitchell, Bob. "Biochemist Har Gobind Khorana, Whose UW Work Earned the Nobel Prize, Dies." University of Wisconsin–Madison News, November 11, 2011. https://news.wisc.edu/biochemist-har-go-bind-khorana-whose-uw-work-earned-the-nobel-prize-dies/.
"Remembering Biochemist Har Gobind Khorana on His 100th Birth Anniversary." *The Wire Science*, September 1, 2022. https://science .thewire.in/society/history/remembering-biochemist-har-gobind -khorana-on-his-100th-birth-anniversary/.
Sakmar, Thomas P. "Har Gobind Khorana." *Proceedings of the American Philosophical Society* 161, no. 3 (September 2017).

Adda Howie
Larson, Kathryn. "Darlington Gelato Store Shares Scoop on Female Dairy Industry Pioneer." Spectrum News 1, March 11, 2021. https:// spectrumnews1.com/wi/milwaukee/news/2021/03/11/taste-of-a -trailblazer--darlington-gelato-store-shares-scoop-on-female-dairy -industry-pioneer.

Margaret H'Doubler
H'Doubler, Margaret. *Dance: A Creative Art Experience*. Madison: University of Wisconsin Press, 1998.

Notes

Preface
1. Edna Ferber, "Is Master of Locks and Bolts," *Appleton Evening Crescent*, July 21, 1904.

The Beatles
1. Dean Robbins, "Milwaukee Meets the Beatles," *Wisconsin Life*, Wisconsin Public Radio, May 30, 2019, https://wisconsinlife.org/story/milwaukee-meets-the-beatles/.

Elvis Presley
1. Thomas W. Still, "Elvis in Town in Time to Halt East Side Fight," *Wisconsin State Journal*, June 25, 1977.

Liberace
1. Darden Asbury Pyron, *Liberace: An American Boy* (Chicago: University of Chicago, 2000), 288.
2. Nathan Bierma, "You Can Take This Cliché to the Bank," *Chicago Tribune*, March 12, 2008, www.chicagotribune.com/2008/03/12/you-can-take-this-cliche-to-the-bank/.

Bob Dylan
1. Stuart D. Levitan, *Madison in the Sixties* (Madison: Wisconsin Historical Society Press, 2018).
2. James B. Nelson, "Bob Dylan's Handwritten Ode to Wisconsin from 1961 Draws No Bids," *Milwaukee Journal Sentinel*, March 30, 2017, www.jsonline.com/story/news/local/milwaukee/2017/03/30/bob-dylans-handwritten-ode-wisconsin-1961-draws-no-bids/99841394/.

Duke Ellington
1. Edward Green, ed., *The Cambridge Companion to Duke Ellington* (Cambridge, England: Cambridge University Press, 2015).
2. Duke Ellington, *Music Is My Mistress* (Garden City, NY: Doubleday, 1973).

Woody Herman
1. Jack Jones, "Woody Herman Dies at 74 after Half Century of Making Swing Music," *Los Angeles Times*, October 30, 1987.

Frank Morgan

1. "Remembering Frank Morgan," *Fresh Air with Terry Gross*, WHYY, December 18, 2007, https://freshairarchive.org/segments/remembe ring-jazz-saxophonist-frank-morgan.
2. "Remembering Frank Morgan."
3. Dean Robbins, "The Saxman Cometh," *Milwaukee Magazine* 20, no. 5 (May 1995).

Viola Smith

1. Viola Smith, "Give Girl Musicians a Break!" *Down Beat*, February 1, 1942.

Roscoe Mitchell

1. Roscoe Mitchell, interview with the author, 1984, Madison, Wisconsin.

Lynda Barry

1. "Lynda Barry," Fellows, MacArthur Foundation, published on September 25, 2019, www.macfound.org/fellows/class-of-2019/lynda-barry.

The Ringling Brothers

1. Jerry Apps, *Tents, Tigers, and the Ringling Brothers* (Madison: Wisconsin Historical Society Press, 2007).
2. Apps, *Tents, Tigers, and the Ringling Brothers*.
3. David Montgomery and Kelly McCullough, "Albert C. Ringling," Immigrant Entrepreneurship, www.immigrantentrepreneurship .org/entries/albert-c-ringling/.
4. Montgomery and McCullough, "Albert C. Ringling."
5. Apps, *Tents, Tigers, and the Ringling Brothers*.
6. Apps, *Tents, Tigers, and the Ringling Brothers*.

Lorraine Hansberry

1. Imani Perry, *Looking for Lorraine: The Radiant and Radical Life of Lorraine Hansberry* (Boston: Beacon Press, 2018).
2. Perry, *Looking for Lorraine*.
3. Perry, *Looking for Lorraine*.

Dickey Chapelle

1. Kevin Ames, "On Photography: Dickey Chapelle, 1918–1965," *Photofocus*, https://photofocus.com/inspiration/on-photography-dickey -chapelle-1918-1965/.
2. Nina Strochlic, "Inside the Daring Life of a Forgotten Female War Photographer," *National Geographic*, August 17, 2018, www.national geographic.com/culture/article/world-photography-day-dickey -chapelle-female-war-photographer-combat-vietnam.
3. Meg Waite Clayton, "The Women Who Fought to Be War Correspondents," *Los Angeles Times*, November 10, 2015, https://www.latimes

.com/opinion/op-ed/la-oe-clayton-female-war-correspondents-20151110-story.html.

Eudora Welty

1. "Welty's World," *Washington Post*, April 4, 1984.
2. Eudora Welty, *One Writer's Beginnings* (Cambridge, MA: Harvard University Press, 1984).
3. Welty, *One Writer's Beginnings*.

Orson Welles

1. Duane Dudek, "Orson Welles' Complicated Feelings for Kenosha," *Milwaukee Journal Sentinel*, October 25, 2008, https://archive.jsonline .com/entertainment/movies/33095059.html.
2. Patrick McGilligan, *Young Orson: The Years of Luck and Genius on the Path to* Citizen Kane (New York: Harper, 2015).
3. Stu Levitan, "Lowell Frautschi Sets the Record Straight on Orson Welles' Time in Madison," *Isthmus*, August 8, 2013.
4. Orson Welles, "War of the Worlds" radio broadcast, 1938, www.youtube .com/watch?v=XsoK4ApWl4g.

Kevin Henkes and Laura Dronzek

1. Kevin Henkes and Laura Dronzek, interview with the author, Madison, Wisconsin, June 23, 2023.

Beth Nguyen

1. Bich Minh Nguyen, *Stealing Buddha's Dinner: A Memoir* (New York: Viking, 2007).
2. Beth Nguyen, *Owner of a Lonely Heart* (New York: Scribner, 2023).

Edna Ferber

1. "Edna Ferber, Novelist, 82, Dies," *New York Times*, April 17, 1968.
2. Edna Ferber, "Is Master of Locks and Bolts," *Appleton Evening Crescent*, July 21, 1904.
3. Julie Goldsmith Gilbert, *Ferber: A Biography* (Garden City, NY: Doubleday, 1978).
4. Gilbert, *Ferber*.

Joyce Carol Oates

1. Joyce Carol Oates, *Marya: A Life* (New York, Dutton, 1986).
2. Joyce Carol Oates, "Nighthawk: Recollections of a Lost Time," in *The Lost Landscape: A Writer's Coming of Age* (New York: Ecco, 2015).
3. Oates, "Nighthawk."
4. Oates, "Nighthawk."
5. Oates, "Nighthawk."

Helen Farnsworth Mears

1. Louise Collier Willcox, "A Notable Woman Sculptor," *Harper's Weekly*, June 20, 1908.

2. "Badger Sculptress Dead in New York," *Madison Democrat*, February 19, 1916.

Lorine Niedecker

1. August Kleinzahler, "This Condensery," *London Review of Books* 25, no. 11 (June 2003), www.lrb.co.uk/the-paper/v25/n11/august-kleinzahler/this-condensery.

2. Kleinzahler, "This Condensery."

3. Lorine Niedecker, *Lorine Niedecker: Collected Works*, ed. Jenny Penberthy (Berkeley: University of California Press, 2002).

Zona Gale

1. "Death Claims Zona Gale Breese, Wisconsin Writer, Civil Leader," *Wisconsin State Journal*, December 28, 1938.

2. "Zona Gale's First Story Brought $3—and Joy," *Wisconsin State Journal*, December 28, 1938.

3. "Death Claims Zona Gale Breese."

Avi

1. Avi, interview with the author, Steamboat Springs, Colorado, April 6, 2021.

Chris Farley

1. Marianne Garvey, "Adam Sandler Still Gets Emotional Singing Sweet Chris Farley Song," CNN, December 5, 2022, www.cnn.com/2022/12/05/entertainment/adam-sandler-chris-farley-song-snl/index.html.

Oprah Winfrey

1. "The Best Christmas of Oprah's Life," *The Oprah Winfrey Show*, 2003, www.oprah.com/oprahshow/the-christmas-that-gave-oprah-hope-video.

Meinhardt Raabe

1. Dee Dunheim, "Meinhardt Raabe, Coroner," The Indiana Wizard of Oz Festival, https://wizardofozfestival.tripod.com/raabe.html.

2. Dunheim, "Meinhardt Raabe."

3. Jay Rath, "Big Dreams: Meinhardt Raabe's Journey Takes Him from Madison to Hollywood and Back, by Way of the Yellow Brick Road," *Wisconsin State Journal*, December 16, 2005, https://madison.com/lifestyles/big-dreams-meinhardt-raabes-journey-takes-him-from-madison-to-hollywood-and-back-by-way/article_967ea1f1-e687-5513-abeb-8b3672f30066.html.

Charlie Hill

1. Charlie Hill on *The Richard Pryor Show*, 1977, YouTube video, www .youtube.com/watch?v=kFSoWpYjkzc.
2. Kliph Nesteroff, "How Charlie Hill Became the First Native Standup Comedy Star," *Esquire*, February 11, 2021, www.esquire.com/enter tainment/books/a35446676/charlie-hill-native-comedian/.
3. Charlie Hill at the Winnipeg Comedy Festival, 2005, YouTube video, www.youtube.com/watch?v=R6gu-t2lPCA.

Fred MacMurray

1. *TV Guide*, July 31, 1965.
2. Frank Judge, "Judging It," *Detroit News*, December 1974.
3. Charles Tranberg, *Fred MacMurray: A Biography* (Albany, GA: Bear-Manor Media, 2007), 155.
4. Ed Sikov, *On Sunset Boulevard: The Life and Times of Billy Wilder* (New York: Hyperion, 1998), 438.

Agnes Moorehead

1. "Agnes Moorehead," City of Reedsburg, Wisconsin, www.reedsburgwi .gov/index.asp?SEC=F4929A3E-5508-478A-9599-29714D684216&DE =A5D9BA25-5281-463A-89AC-A38159549333.

Hattie McDaniel

1. Hattie McDaniel, "Hattie McDaniel Defies Critics in 1947 Essay: 'I Have Never Apologized,'" *Hollywood Reporter*, February 19, 2015, www .hollywoodreporter.com/movies/movie-news/hattie-mcdaniel-defies -critics-1947-774493/.
2. McDaniel, "Hattie McDaniel."
3. Hadley Hall Meares, "The Icon and the Outcast: Hattie McDaniel's Epic Double Life," *Vanity Fair*, April 26, 2021, www.vanityfair.com /hollywood/2021/04/hattie-mcdaniel-gone-with-the-wind-oscars -autobiography.

Allen Ludden

1. Greta Bjornson, "Carol Burnett Recalls Betty White's 'Great Love' with Late Husband Allen Ludden," *People*, December 31, 2021, https://peo- ple.com/movies/why-remarry-when-you-had-the-best-carol -burnett-recalls-betty-whites-romance-with-allen-ludden/.

Carrie Coon

1. Kenneth Burns, "Star Quality," *Isthmus*, June 16, 2006.

Willem Dafoe

1. Shane Nyman, "8 Times Appleton Native Willem Dafoe Appeared in *The Post-Crescent* before He Was Famous," *Appleton Post-Crescent*,

January 17, 2019, www.postcrescent.com/story/entertainment/2019
/01/17/willem-dafoe-8-times-actor-appleton-newspaper-before
-getting-famous/2569510002/.

2. Shane Nyman, "Willem Dafoe Talks Appleton Upbringing on 'WTF'
Podcast," *Appleton Post-Crescent*, October 25, 2017, www.postcrescent.
com/story/entertainment/2017/10/25/willem-dafoe-talks-appleton
-upbringing-wtf-podcast/793778001/.

3. Audrey Nowakowski, "Actor Willem Dafoe Reflects on UW–
Milwaukee's Part in His Development as a Performer," WUWM,
May 24, 2022, www.wuwm.com/2022-05-24/actor-willem-dafoe
-reflects-on-uw-milwaukees-part-in-his-development-as-a-performer.

4. John Schneider, "Willem Dafoe: The Oscar-Nominated Actor Remembers His Time at UWM and Milwaukee's Theatre X," *MKElifestyle*,
February 17, 2023, www.mkelifestyle.com/artsandculture/willem
-dafoe/article_de92f874-ae56-11ed-bcfb-efa9d2d2c511.html.

5. John Schumacher, "An Actor's Homecoming: Willem Dafoe Returns
to Where It All Started," *UWM Report*, June 17, 2022, https://uwm
.edu/news/an-actors-homecoming-willem-dafoe-returns-to-where
-it-all-started/.

6. Willem Dafoe Monologue, *Saturday Night Live*, January 29, 2022,
www.youtube.com/watch?v=xAOuAlG5jJM.

André De Shields

1. Jenny Price, "The One and Only André De Shields," *On Wisconsin*,
Winter 2019.

2. André De Shields 2019 Tony Award Speech, YouTube video, www.you
tube.com/watch?v=nHIYYqmL_TY.

Mary Hinkson

1. Anna Kisselgoff, "Mary Hinkson, a Star for Martha Graham, Dies at 89,"
New York Times, November 28, 2014, www.nytimes.com/2014/11/30
/arts/dance/-mary-hinkson-a-star-for-martha-graham-dies-at-89.html.

Alfred Lunt and Lynn Fontanne

1. Alden Whitman, "Always Working," *New York Times*, August 4, 1977.

2. "The Guest List," Ten Chimneys, www.tenchimneys.org/about/the
-guest-list.

Uta Hagen

1. Uta Hagen, *Sources: A Memoir* (New York: Performing Arts Journal
Publications, 1983).

2. Hagen, *Sources*.

Jackie Robinson

1. Ron Rabinovitz, "More Than Just #42," Simply A Fan, July 16, 2018, www.simplyafan.com/2018/07/more-than-just-42/.
2. Do-Hyoung Park, "JR and the Kid: Unlikely Bond Spans Decades," MLB.com, April 15, 2021, www.mlb.com/news/jackie-robinson -friendship-with-ron-rabinovitz.

Bart Starr

1. Jim Banks, "Bart Starr: A Legendary Quarterback," *Sports Illustrated*, May 7, 2020, www.si.com/college/alabama/football/bart-starr -alabama-football-crimson-tide-football-green-bay-packers-super -bowl.
2. William Yardley, "Bart Starr, Quarterback Who Led the Packers to Greatness, Dies at 85," *New York Times*, May 26, 2019, www.nytimes .com/2019/05/26/obituaries/bart-starr-death-packers.html.
3. Zak Keefer, "NFL 100: At No. 61, Bart Starr Made the Blueprint for Brett Favre, Aaron Rodgers, Tom Brady and More," *The Athletic*, July 28, 2021, https://theathletic.com/2644572/2021/07/28/nfl-100 -at-no-62-bart-starr-made-the-blueprint-for-brett-favre-aaron-rodgers -tom-brady-and-more/.
4. "50 Years Ago: The 'Ice Bowl,'" NFL Communications, https://nflcom munications.com/Pages/50-Years-Ago--The-Ice-Bowl.aspx.

Mark Johnson

1. "Russians Trounce U.S. Hockey Team," Associated Press, February 10, 1980.
2. Eric Barrow, "Step Out on the Ice with Mark Johnson, the Unsung Miracle Man of the 1980 U.S. Hockey Team," *New York Daily News*, February 21, 2015, www.nydailynews.com/2015/02/21/step-out-on -the-ice-with-mark-johnson-the-unsung-miracle-man-of-the-1980 -us-hockey-team/.
3. Ed Graney, "Mark Johnson Was Understated Star of Miracle on Ice Team," *Las Vegas Review-Journal*, February 18, 2020, www.reviewjour nal.com/sports/goldenknights/mark-johnson-was-understated-star -of-miracle-on-ice-team-1960079/.

Hank Aaron

1. Jerry Poling, *A Summer Up North: Henry Aaron and the Legend of Eau Claire Baseball* (Madison: University of Wisconsin Press, 2002).
2. Poling, *A Summer Up North*.

Eric and Beth Heiden

1. "The Heidens," *Washington Post*, February 10, 1980.
2. Mike Rowbottom, "Heiden's Own Miracle on Ice Still Resonates in Olympic History 40 Years On," Inside the Games, February 23, 2020, www.insidethegames.biz/articles/1090904/eric-heiden-speed-skating-olympics.
3. JR Radcliffe, "50 in 50: Eric Heiden Wins Fifth Gold Medal at 1980 Olympics," *Milwaukee Journal Sentinel*, May 13, 2020, www.jsonline.com/story/sports/olympics/2020/05/13/50-greatest-wisconsin-sports-moments-no-10-eric-heiden/3070257001/.
4. Radcliffe, "50 in 50."

The Racine Belles and Kenosha Comets

1. "Rules of Conduct," All-American Girls Professional Baseball League, www.aagpbl.org/history/rules-of-conduct.
2. Jack Fincher, "AAGPBL History: The 'Belles of the Ball Game' Were a Hit with Their Fans," All-American Girls Professional Baseball League, www.aagpbl.org/articles/show/39.
3. Joyce Barnes McCoy, "McCoy, Joyce Barnes (Interview transcript and video), September 27, 2009," Digital Collections, Grand Valley State University, https://digitalcollections.library.gvsu.edu/document/29685.

Kareem Abdul-Jabbar

1. Thomas Bonk, "A Banner Day for Lakers: Kareem Takes His Post," *Los Angeles Times*, December 25, 1987.
2. Bradshaw Furlong, "Milwaukee Bucks: Kareem Abdul-Jabbar Calls City His 'Place of Birth,'" Behind the Buck Pass, September 15, 2021, https://behindthebuckpass.com/2021/09/15/milwaukee-bucks-kareem-abdul-jabbar-calls-city-place-birth/.
3. Greg Moore, "Kareem Abdul-Jabbar Laughs First, but Phoenix Suns Fans Laugh Best after Game 2 Win," *Arizona Republic*, July 8, 2021, www.azcentral.com/story/sports/nba/suns/2021/07/08/kareem-abdul-jabbar-talks-trash-phoenix-suns-respond-thumping-milwaukee-bucks-nba-finals/7909911002/.

Kit Saunders-Nordeen

1. Doug Moe, *The Right Thing to Do: Kit Saunders-Nordeen and the Rise of Women's Intercollegiate Athletics at the University of Wisconsin and Beyond* (Milwaukee, WI: HenschelHAUS Publishing, 2022).
2. Martin Luther King Jr., *Letter from Birmingham Jail* (London: Penguin UK, 2018).

George Poage

1. Bruce L. Mouser, *George Coleman Poage—1880–1962: America's First African American Olympic Medalist: A Biography* (La Crosse, WI: self-published ebook, 2017).

Gwen Jorgensen

1. Lindsay Crouse, "Gwen Jorgensen Tries to Solve the Marathon," *New York Times*, October 5, 2018, www.nytimes.com/2018/10/05/sports/olympics/gwen-jorgensen-olympic-marathon.html.

Jim Lovell

1. Jim Lovell and Jeffrey Kluger, *Apollo 13* (Boston: Mariner Books, 2006).
2. James Lovell, interview with the author, Madison, Wisconsin, April 30, 2020.
3. Lovell, interview with the author.

Jeffrey Erlanger

1. "A Visit with Jeff Erlanger," *Mister Rogers' Neighborhood*, https://misterrogers.org/articles/jeffrey-erlanger/.
2. John Stofflet, "Making a Difference: Memory of Madison Man Who Inspired Mister Rogers Inspires Expansion of Accessible Playgrounds in Madison," WMTV, May 27, 2021, www.wmtv15news.com/2021/05/27/making-a-difference-memory-of-madison-man-who-inspired-mr-rogers-inspires-expansion-of-accessible-playgrounds-in-madison/.
3. Fred Rogers Hall of Fame Induction, Television Academy, www.emmys.com/video/fred-rogers-hall-fame-induction-1999.

Joshua Glover

1. Joseph A. Scolaro, "Joshua Glover: Runaway Slave in Racine Made Legal History," *Journal Times* (Racine), May 29, 1998.
2. Margo Kirchner, "Unsung Hero: Joshua Glover—His Escape from Slavery and the Law Sparked State Abolitionist Action," Wisconsin Justice Initiative, December 3, 2021, www.wjiinc.org/blog/unsung-hero-joshua-glover-his-escapes-from-slavery-and-the-law-sparked-state-abolitionist-action.
3. Ruby West Jackson and Walter T. McDonald, *Finding Freedom: The Untold Story of Joshua Glover, Freedom Seeker* (Madison: Wisconsin Historical Society Press, 2022).
4. Henry E. Legler, "Rescue of Joshua Glover, A Runaway Slave," *Leading Events of Wisconsin History* (Milwaukee: The Sentinel Company, 1898), 226–229, https://digicoll.library.wisc.edu/WIReader/WER1124.html.

Mountain Wolf Woman and Nancy Oestreich Lurie

1. Mountain Wolf Woman, *Mountain Wolf Woman, Sister of Crashing Thunder: The Autobiography of a Winnebago Indian*, ed. Nancy Oestreich Lurie (Ann Arbor: University of Michigan Press, 1961).

Hans Christian Heg

1. Theodore C. Blegen, "Colonel Hans Christian Heg," *Wisconsin Magazine of History* 4, no. 2 (December 1920): 140–165.
2. Blegen, "Colonel Hans Christian Heg."
3. Blegen, "Colonel Hans Christian Heg."

Laurel Clark

1. Cristina Daglas and Sara Zurn, "Columbia Disaster Hits Home," *Badger Herald*, February 3, 2003.
2. "Bio: Shuttle Columbia Physician Cmdr. Dr. Laurel Clark," Fox News, January 13, 2015, www.foxnews.com/story/bio-shuttle-columbia -physician-cmdr-dr-laurel-clark.
3. Daglas and Zurn, "Columbia Disaster Hits Home."
4. "'Hello From Above Our Magnificent Planet Earth,'" *Guardian*, February 3, 2003, www.theguardian.com/science/2003/feb/03/space exploration.columbia11.

Ada Deer

1. Ada Deer, *Making a Difference: My Fight for Native Rights and Social Justice* (Norman: University of Oklahoma Press, 2019).
2. Deer, *Making a Difference*.
3. Deer, *Making a Difference*.

Caroline Quarlls

1. Michael Edmonds and Samantha Snyder, *Warriors, Saints, and Scoundrels: Brief Portraits of Real People Who Shaped Wisconsin* (Madison: Wisconsin Historical Society Press, 2017), 139.
2. Julia Pferdehirt, *Caroline Quarlls and the Underground Railroad* (Madison: Wisconsin Historical Society Press, 2008).

Edward Berner, George Hallauer, and the Girl from Two Rivers

1. Michelle York, "The Ice Cream Sundae's Birthplace? That's the 64,000-Calorie Question," *New York Times*, August 6, 2006, www .nytimes.com/2006/08/06/nyregion/06sundae.html.

Kathryn Clarenbach

1. Ellen Chesler, "Lives Well Lived: Kathryn F. Clarenbach; Now, Then," *New York Times*, January 1, 1995, www.nytimes.com/1995/01/01 /magazine/lives-well-lived-kathryn-f-clarenbach-now-then.html.

Electa Quinney

1. Karen Saemann, *Electa Quinney: Stockbridge Teacher* (Madison: Wisconsin Historical Society Press, 2014).

Vel Phillips

1. Richard Sandomir, "Vel Phillips, Housing Rights Champion in the '60s, Is Dead at 95," *New York Times*, April 25, 2018, www.nytimes.com/2018/04/25/obituaries/vel-phillips-housing-rights-champion-in-the-60s-dies-at-95.html.

2. James R. Hagerty, "Vel Phillips Fought Six Years to Allow Blacks to Live Where They Wished," *Wall Street Journal*, May 4, 2018, www.wsj.com/articles/vel-phillips-fought-six-years-to-allow-blacks-to-live-where-they-wished-1525385413.

3. Sandomir, "Vel Phillips."

4. Lainey Seyler, "Everything You Want to Know about Vel Phillips That's Probably Not in a History Book," *Milwaukee Journal Sentinel*, April 18, 2018, www.jsonline.com/story/communities/south/news/south-milwaukee/2018/04/18/interesting-facts-vel-phillips-who-trailblazer-civil-rights-here-some-more-interesting-facts-her-lif/527807002/.

Belle Case La Follette

1. Nancy C. Unger, "The Two Worlds of Belle Case La Follette," *Wisconsin Magazine of History* 83, no. 2 (Winter 1999–2000): 82–110.

2. Nancy C. Unger, "The Unexpected Belle La Follette," *Wisconsin Magazine of History* 99, no. 3 (Spring 2016): 16–27.

3. Nancy C. Unger, "Legacies of Belle La Follette's Big Tent Campaigns for Women's Suffrage," *American Journalism* 36, no. 1 (2019): 51–70, www.tandfonline.com/doi/abs/10.1080/08821127.2019.1572412.

4. Unger, "Unexpected Belle La Follette."

5. Unger, "Unexpected Belle La Follette."

Jesus Salas

1. Jesus Salas, "Three Generations of Migrant Workers," Madison Area Technical College Intercultural Exchange, September 27, 2018, YouTube video, www.youtube.com/watch?v=DYsr6bBbWKo.

Marianne Labuche

1. James H. Lockwood, "Early Times and Events in Wisconsin," Second Annual Report and Collections of the State Historical Society of Wisconsin for the Year 1855 (Madison: Calkins & Proudfit, 1856): 98–196, www.wisconsinhistory.org/turningpoints/search.asp?id=30.

2. "Woman First State 'Doctor,'" *Milwaukee Sunday Journal*, November 29, 1925.

3. Earl R. Thayer, "First in Their Class: Wisconsin's Pioneering Women Physicians," *Wisconsin Academy Review* 51, no. 2 (Spring 2005): 51–62.

Aldo Leopold

1. Aldo Leopold, *A Sand County Almanac: And Sketches Here and There* (London, New York: Oxford University Press, 1949).

Harriet Bell Merrill

1. Sandra Knisely Barnidge, "These Boots Were Made for History," *On Wisconsin*, Summer 2022.
2. Merrillyn L. Hartridge, *The Anandrous Journey: Revealing Letters to a Mentor* (Amherst, WI: Amherst Press, 1997).
3. Hartridge, *The Anandrous Journey.*
4. Hartridge, *The Anandrous Journey.*
5. Hartridge, *The Anandrous Journey.*
6. "Enjoyed a Long Trip: Harriet Bell Returns from a Trip to South America," *Virginia Enterprise*, December 5, 1902.
7. Hartridge, *The Anandrous Journey.*

Ann Landers and Abigail Van Buren

1. Andrew Dowd, " 'Abby' Fondly Recalled Her Years in Eau Claire," *Leader-Telegram* (Eau Claire), January 17, 2013, www.leadertelegram.com/news/front-page/abby-fondly-recalled-her-years-in-eau-claire/article_50823499-b9a5-51ba-a1c0-e33e30abe875.html.
2. "Twin Lovelorn Advisors Torn Asunder by Success," *Life*, April 7, 1958.

Esther Lederberg

1. Katy Steinmetz, "Why Don't We Remember More Trailblazing Women Scientists?," *Time*, April 11, 2019, https://time.com/longform/esther-lederberg/.
2. Steinmetz, "Esther Lederberg."

Will Allen

1. Will Allen, with Charles Wilson, *The Good Food Revolution: Growing Healthy Food, People, and Communities* (New York: Gotham Books, 2012).
2. Daniel Simmons, "We Chatted with Will Allen after His Ugly Public Divorce from Growing Power," *Milwaukee Magazine*, October 9, 2018, www.milwaukeemag.com/will-allen-after-growing-power-defunct/.
3. Stephen Satterfield, "Behind the Rise and Fall of Growing Power," Civil Eats, March 13, 2018, https://civileats.com/2018/03/13/behind-the-rise-and-fall-of-growing-power/.

Sigurd Olson

1. Sigurd Olson, *The Singing Wilderness* (New York: Knopf, 1956).
2. Sigurd Olson, Wisconsin Conservation Hall of Fame, https://wchf .org/sigurd-olson/.
3. Greg Seitz, "Sigurd Olson's Writing Shack Designated a Historic Site of National Significance," *Quetico Superior Wilderness News*, December 12, 2020, https://queticosuperior.org/sigurd-olsons-writing -shack-designated-a-historic-site-of-national-significance.

Har Gobind Khorana

1. Alok A. Khorana, "Dr. Har Gobind Khorana at 100: Reevaluating a Shared Heritage," *Dawn*, January 8, 2022, www.dawn.com/news /1668120.

Adda Howie

1. George H. Dacy, "America's Outstanding Woman Farmer," *Forecast*, April 1925, folder 3, Adda F. Howie Collection, Wisconsin Historical Society Archives, Madison, Wisconsin.
2. Thomas Ramstack, *Brookfield and Elm Grove* (Mount Pleasant, SC: Arcadia Publishing, 2009), 109.
3. Nancy Unger, "Adda F. Howie: 'America's Outstanding Woman Farmer,'" *Wisconsin Magazine of History* 100, no. 4 (Summer 2017): 40–45.

Margaret H'Doubler

1. "Margaret H'Doubler and the Wisconsin Dance Idea," in "Health and Fun Shall Walk Hand in Hand": The First 100 Years of Women's Athletics at UW–Madison, University of Wisconsin–Madison Libraries, www.library.wisc.edu/archives/exhibits/campus-history-projects /health-and-fun-shall-walk-hand-in-hand-the-first-100-years-of -womens-athletics-at-uw-madison/margaret-hdoubler-and-the -wisconsin-dance-idea/.
2. Judith Anne Gray, *To Want to Dance: A Biography of Margaret H'Doubler* (University of Arizona dissertation, 1978).
3. Gray, *To Want to Dance*.

Chia Youyee Vang

1. Chia Youyee Vang, *Hmong America: Reconstructing Community in Diaspora* (Urbana: University of Illinois Press, 2010).

Index

Page numbers in *italics* refer to images.

Nitschke, Ray, 163
Nobel Prize, 251, 252, 260, 261–262
Northern Exposure, 7
Northland College, 259
Norway, 206

Oak Creek, 253
Oates, Joyce Carol, 80–82
Oates, Warren, 255
Obreros Unidos (United Workers), 232
O'Casey, Sean, 59
O'Keeffe, Georgia, 72–73
Olson, Sigurd, 258–259
Olympic Games, 164–166, 171, 183, 185, 186
"On, Wisconsin," 20, 119
Onion, the, 239–241
Orchesis, 148, 267–268
Oriental Theatre, 60
Osborn, Jinny, 11–13, *12*
Oscar Mayer corporation, 112–113
Oscars. *See* Academy Awards
Oshkosh, 88, 96
Oshkosh State Normal School, 88, 89
Osseo, 8
Our Lady Queen of Peace Church, 109
Owner of a Lonely Heart (Nguyen), 76

Pabst Theater, 16
Pail and Shovel Party, 239
Paramount, 40, 41
Parker, Charlie, 35
Password, 132
Pasteur Award, 252
Patton, Charley, 40
Paul, Alice, 179, 230
Paul, Les, 42–44, *43*
Peck, Gregory, 151
PEN/Hemingway Award for Debut Novel, 87
Pepin, 269
Phillips, Vel, 225–227, *226*
Phoenix Suns, 176, 178
Picnic Point, 156, 200, 201
Piper, Carly, 181
Poage, George, 182–183
Political Equality League of Wisconsin, 221
Portage, 97, 98–99

Poynette, 55
Prairie du Chien, 54, 234, 236
Prentice, 258
Presidential Medal of Freedom, 63
Presley, Elvis, 9–10, 12
Primrose, 228
Pryor, Richard, 116. See also *Richard Pryor Show*
Public Enemies (2009), 96
Pulitzer Prize, 63, 77, 98

Quarlls, Caroline, 215–216
Quinney, Electa, 223–224
Quintana, Ricardo, 64

Raabe, Meinhardt, 112–114, *113*
Rabinovitz, Ronnie, 159–161
Racine, 69, 118, 174, 197, 198, 208, 209
Racine Belles, 173–175
Racine County, 86, 198
Raisin in the Sun, A (Hansberry), 58, 59
Rawhide Boys Ranch, 163
Red Barn Theater, 122
Red Orchestra, 201
Red Rooster Cafe, 132
Redcloud, Mitchell, Sr., 202
Redding, Otis, 33–34
Reedsburg, 124
Renaissance Theatreworks, 139
Rice Lake, 156
Richard Pryor Show, 115, 116–117
Richland Center, 51, 83, 221, 222
Richland Center Woman's Club, 221
Riggs, Bobby, 179
Ringling, Al, 54, 56, *56*
Ringling, Alfred, 54, 56, *56*
Ringling, Charles, 54, 56, *56*
Ringling, Gus, 55, 56
Ringling, Henry, 55, 56
Ringling, John, 54, 56, *56*
Ringling, Otto, 54, 56, *56*
Ringling Brothers, 54–57
Ripon College, 122, 123, 144, 145
Ripon Weekly Press, 145
River Falls, 55
Robinson, Edward G., *120*
Robinson, Jackie, 159–161, *160*, 182
Robinson, Rachel, 160
Rochester, 86, 198

About the Author

Dean Robbins is a journalist, arts critic, and children's author. He has contributed to *USA Today*, *The New York Daily News*, *The Village Voice*, Space.com, the Grammys magazine, Wisconsin Public Radio, and dozens of other media outlets, along with serving as editor of *Isthmus* newspaper and *On Wisconsin* magazine. His nonfiction children's books—including *The Faster Drummer: Clap Your Hands for Viola Smith!* and *Margaret and the Moon: How Margaret Hamilton Saved the First Lunar Landing*—have been praised in the *New York Times*, *Los Angeles Times*, *USA Today*, and *Wall Street Journal*; chosen for best-of-the-year honors by the American Library Association, New York Public Library, Chicago Public Library, and others; adapted for audiobooks and film; and featured in a Smithsonian exhibition. Dean has won both national and state awards for news writing, feature writing, arts writing, and children's books.

PHOTO BY DAVID GIROUX